W9-AXC-371

HEARTLAND COOKING
CASSEROLES

HEARTLAND COOKING

CASSEROLES

FRANCES TOWNER GIEDT

PHOTOGRAPHS BY
Eleanor Thompson

Reader's
Digest

The Reader's Digest Association, Inc.
Pleasantville, New York/Montreal

A Reader's Digest Book

CONCEIVED AND PRODUCED BY
Miller and O'Shea, Inc.

DESIGNED BY
Lisa Billard Design

The acknowledgments that appear on page 5 are hereby made a part of this copyright page.

Library of Congress Cataloging in Publication Data
Giedt, Frances Towner.
    Casseroles / Frances Towner Giedt ; photographs by Eleanor Thompson.
        p. cm. — (Heartland cooking)
    Includes index.
    ISBN 0-89577-878-5
     1. Casserole cookery. 2. Cookery, American—Midwestern style.
  I. Title   II. Series.
  TX693.G54 1996
  641.8'21—dc20   96-7248

Printed in the United States of America

DEDICATED

TO THE GIRLS —

Jackie and Kim

ACKNOWLEDGMENTS

WRITING CASSEROLES WOULD NOT HAVE BEEN POSSIBLE WITHOUT THE HELP AND GENEROSITY of some very special and talented friends and associates.

I'm grateful to my friend Eleanor Thompson who photographed everything so exquisitely and to her assistant, Chris Hobson. Many thanks also to Paul E. Piccuito for his excellent food styling and to Lori Benton for creatively propping each photo.

Among those responsible for this book, a special thanks to Angela Miller and Coleen O'Shea, whose inspired idea it was; to Lisa Billard for her beautiful book design; and to Kathy Kingsley and Chris Benton for their helpful and careful editing.

My sincere gratitude to the following shops and stores that generously let us borrow extensively from their shelves for the photography of the recipes: Anka, Darien, CT; The Complete Kitchen, Darien, CT; Forgotten Garden, Wilton, CT; LCR, Westport, CT; Pottery Barn; Villa Ceramica, South Norwalk, CT; and Williams-Sonoma. Many other items came from the private collections of friends and associates. I thank you all.

Last, but not least, my love and appreciation to my family and friends who came forth with recipes and encouragement — and especially to my husband, David, for his untiring support, inspiration, or just a great night out when I needed it.

CONT

E N T S

UCH OF MY CHILDHOOD WAS SPENT IN MY MOTHER'S
kitchen. Knowing that she would be baking something or
cooking dinner, I went there the moment I got home from
school. First I'd enjoy a snack she'd have waiting, then
she'd sit down to hear about my day.

I can remember a particular time as if it were yesterday, sitting at the
breakfast bar in that cozy room looking out onto our big screened porch,
excitedly relating that my eighth grade teacher had submitted my short
story to a Kansas City magazine and they'd agreed to publish it—and someday I was going be a famous writer.
My mother smiled and suggested that maybe I'd better decide what kind of writing I wanted to do and set a course
of study toward that end. In a heartbeat I responded that I
wanted to become a foreign correspondent and write about important changes in the world, a notion that held fast until I en-
rolled in the school of journalism at Kansas State University.

INTRO

As a freshman I was required to attend a series of seminars given by former graduates who had achieved con-
siderable stature as journalists. The last of those seminars was led by Clementine Paddleford, food editor of the *New
York Herald Tribune*. She inspired me to change my ultimate course of study to one in home economics and jour-

nalism, with a specialty in foods and nutrition. That shifted
the focus of my life's work from writing news stories to writing
about food. Now, some thirty years later, I'm writing about the
food of the thirteen states of America's Heartland —Kansas,
Illinois, Indiana, Iowa, Michigan, Minnesota, Missouri, Ne-
braska, North Dakota, Ohio, Oklahoma, South Dakota, and
Wisconsin. This massive area is the home of the mighty Mississippi River and millions of acres of fertile farmland, and is
the cradle of our great country's home-style cooking.

My maternal grandfather bought his first wheat farm in
Kansas in the late 1800s and began a family tradition of
Kansas wheat farming, a multifarm operation that is still in
business today.

My mother was born and raised on that first farm, and I can remember visiting there as a young child. I was fascinated by the earth-floored root cellar beneath the kitchen wing of the rambling house with its Victorian porches and gingerbread trim. There were bins of flour and cornmeal, ground in the family granary; earthenware crocks of cream-topped milk, freshly churned butter, and homemade cheeses; and jars of home-canned vegetables and meats. Strings of garlic, bundles of onions, and bunches of drying herbs hung from the rafters. The garden down by the creek produced an abundance of fresh vegetables and fruits. Barnyard pigs provided bacon, sausage, and ham, and the henhouse supplied brown-shelled eggs and chicken for Sunday's dinner. Plenty of wild game (pheasant, duck, rabbit, and deer) resided in the fields. Life was not easy, but food was plentiful.

My parents followed this tradition of living off the land. I can remember spending hours on my knees picking up one row and down the other of my father's strawberry field and standing on a chair to help my

mother pluck the feathers from the chicken to use for that night's chicken noodle casserole.

This legacy of cooking from the bounty of the land is at the very heart of Midwestern cuisine — molded by a blend of diverse ethnic influences and an ever-changing store of indigenous foodstuffs, recently augmented by the age of worldwide air freight.

Also at the heart of Heartland cooking is the casserole, a category of dishes so revered by Midwestern cooks that their community cookbooks usually give the dishes a chapter of their own.

The *American Heritage Dictionary* defines casserole as "a dish, usually of earthenware, glass, or cast iron, in which food is both baked and served." In his book *Food and Drink in America*, Richard Hooker describes a casserole as a favorite method of cooking of New World immigrant Italians, Mexicans, Hungarians, and Greeks in the late nineteenth century.

Casseroles are economical, serving the country well during the depressions of the 1890s and 1930s and the rationing of foodstuffs during World War I and II. The birth of commercially canned vegetables in 1903 by the Green Giant Company of Minnesota added to their ease of preparation and made them a vehicle for recycling leftovers and the pride of the church social or neighborhood potluck suppers.

Since the Pillsbury Bake-Off, held since 1949, traditionally gives license to a cook's creativity, nearly 25 percent of the finalists in the contest won for their casserole recipes—a category outdone only by desserts.

Over the years they have been ridiculed as much as they have been loved. Yet who can deny their universal appeal — nothing is easier to make, more humble in concept, or more soul-warming to eat. Casseroles can be thrifty, or they can contain expensive ingredients, worthy of your most sophisticated dinner party guest.

In selecting the recipes for this book, I looked for dishes that are representative of the way people of the Heartland are cooking at home today. I have included an occasional casserole bound in canned soup, since that's how we all actually cook when we're short of time for making a béchamel or other sauce. But you'll also find chicken smothered in pineapple and cheese, onions stuffed with pork and slowly roasted in cream, a recipe for fresh fish of the region, and a quick pizza baked on a bed of angel hair pasta. Meatless selections include a combo of three cheeses and fresh chiles, an oven-baked omelet stuffed with wild mushrooms from the Heartland, and bell peppers stuffed with barley and vegetables.

In the side-dish chapter regional specialties feature native wild rice and other grains, dried cranberries and cherries, plus inventive ways to serve harvest vegetables.

Finally, there's a special chapter of recipes for casseroles to tote to your church social or neighborhood potluck.

In all, there are eighty recipes, most of which can be prepared ahead of time, all of which will inject excitement into the meals you prepare for your family and guests.

FREEZING CASSEROLES Many of the casseroles in this book may be frozen to bake and enjoy later. A recipe that freezes well can be made in duplicate or triplicate, the extra portions cooled quickly, then packed in moisture- and vapor-proof containers, sealed, and frozen for the day you need them. When foods freeze, the organisms that cause spoilage become inactive, but there are some tips to take into account:

• If a casserole contains uncooked rice, uncooked pasta, raw vegetables or raw meat, poultry, or fish that has been previously frozen and thawed, the casserole should be baked before freezing. Most other casseroles can be frozen before baking.

• Add more chili powder and onion than called for in the recipe since these flavors will diminish with freezing. Use less garlic, herbs, green bell pepper, celery, and black pepper since these flavors tend to increase in strength when frozen. Hard-cooked egg whites will become rubbery, and boiled potatoes will darken and change texture when frozen. If a recipe calls for either, add them when you bake or reheat the casserole. Don't freeze a casserole that contains mayonnaise; mayonnaise separates when frozen. Use little or no salt in preparing any casserole for freezing since salt inhibits the freezing process.

• If a casserole is headed for the freezer, leave any topping containing bread crumbs, cracker crumbs, or corn flakes off until it's time to bake or reheat it. This will prevent the topping from becoming soggy. Toppings such as cheese or mashed potatoes freeze well.

• Make sure your freezer temperature is set at 0°F or below to keep the casserole solidly frozen and to

maintain the best food flavor, color, and texture. Use a freezer thermometer to help keep track of the temperature.

• When you add a casserole to the freezer, separate it from the rest of the food packages to allow the cold air to circulate around the casserole until it's frozen solid.

• To keep baking dishes free for cooking, line the casserole dish with a piece of moisture-resistant paper (freezer wrap) or heavy-duty aluminum foil that is large enough to wrap the entire casserole. Fill the dish as directed and cool. Wrap tightly and freeze until firm. Then lift the wrapped food from the dish, label, and return the frozen food to the freezer. When ready to bake, remove the freezer wrap or foil and return the frozen casserole to the baking dish.

• If a casserole contains acidic ingredients such as tomatoes, use moisture-resistant paper (freezer wrap), not aluminum foil.

• Other types of containers suitable for freezing casseroles are rigid plastic containers made specifically for freezer storage and plastic freezer bags.

• Be sure to include the date on the label and check dates regularly to avoid freezing casseroles for longer than 3 to 4 months.

• Generally, frozen unbaked casseroles will take twice as long to bake as freshly made. If an unbaked casserole has been partially defrosted in the refrigerator, cut the baking time slightly. It is always a good idea to check the casserole about 10 to 15 minutes before the end of the stated baking time to prevent overcooking.

• To reheat a frozen already-baked casserole, thaw first in the refrigerator overnight, then reheat at 350°F in the oven just until piping hot. This will help prevent overcooking.

NUTRITIONAL INFORMATION For these recipes the nutritional analysis uses the most current data from "The Food Processor," Version 6.02, by ESHA Research, and the United States Department of Agriculture. Nutritional information is given for calories; grams of protein, total fat and saturated fat, carbohydrates, and dietary fiber; and milligrams of sodium and cholesterol. The nutritional analysis does not include optional ingredients or those for which no specific amount is stated.

METRIC CONVERSION CHART

LIQUID AND DRY MEASURE EQUIVALENTS

Customary	Metric
¼ teaspoon	1.25 milliliters
½ teaspoon	2.5 milliliters
1 teaspoon	5 milliliters
1 tablespoon	15 milliliters
1 fluid ounce	30 milliliters
¼ cup	60 milliliters
⅓ cup	80 milliliters
½ cup	120 milliliters
1 cup	240 milliliters
1 pint (2 cups)	480 milliliters
1 quart (4 cups; 32 ounces)	960 milliliters (.35 liter)
1 gallon (4 quarts)	3.84 liters
1 ounce (by weight)	28.35 grams
¼ pound (4 ounces)	114 grams
1 pound (16 ounces)	454 grams
2.2 pounds	1 kilogram (1,000 grams)

TEMPERATURE EQUIVALENTS

Description	°Fahrenheit	°Celsius
Very cool	200–250	95–120
Cool or slow	275–300	135–150
Warm	325	165
Moderate	350	175
Moderately hot	375	190
Fairly hot	400	200
Hot	425	220
Very hot	450–475	230–245

COOKING AND BAKING EQUIVALENTS

Bakeware	Customary	Metric
Round Pan	8 x 1½ inches	20 x 4 cm
	9 x 1½ inches	23 x 4 cm
	10 x 1½ inches	25 x 4 cm
Square Pan	8 x 8 x 2 inches	20 x 20 x 5 cm
	9 x 9 x 2 inches	23 x 23 x 5 cm
Baking Dishes	7 x 11 x 1½ inches	18 x 28 x 4 cm
	7½ x 12 x 2 inches	19 x 30 x 5 cm
	9 x 13 x 2 inches	23 x 33 x 5 cm
Loaf Pan	4½ x 8½ x 2½ inches	11 x 21 x 6 cm
	5 x 9 x 3 inches	13 x 23 x 8 cm
Casseroles and Saucepans	1 quart	1 liter
	1½ quart	1.5 liter
	2 quart	2 liter
	2½ quart	2.5 liter
	3 quart	3 liter
	4 quart	4 liter

MAIN DISHES

I F YOU HAVE LIVED IN THE HEARTLAND, you are well acquainted with one-dish meals. For most of us the very term casserole or hot dish conjures up memories of chunks of canned tuna, flat egg noodles, maybe some peas — bound together with a can of cream-of-anything soup and topped with a coating of cheese and crushed potato chips — as representative of the Midwest as waving wheat fields.

In this book I have tried to reflect the full range of Heartland cooking. I have included recipes for sundried-tomato–stuffed chicken breasts roasted atop a bed of wild rice, a light-as-a-feather herbed seafood soufflé, a savory mélange of pork and vegetables with a puffy potato crust, and a robust casserole of New York strip steak and wild mushrooms. Some are simpler fare for family meals; others are showstoppers that will enhance any dinner party.

All of the recipes contain basic ingredients to make delicious one-dish meals. I am confident that you will serve these dishes with pride to your family and friends. Some of the casseroles are updated versions of old family recipes; others were developed in my own kitchen, calling for basic ingredients that are indigenous to the Heartland today.

STUFFED CHICKEN BREAST CASSEROLE

MAKES 6 SERVINGS

This is a lovely company dish that calls for fontina, a creamy cheese that melts beautifully inside the chicken breasts. One of Italy's great cheeses, fontina is also made in Wisconsin by Italian-American cheese makers. Swiss cheese or mozzarella can be substituted if you can't find fontina.

1 ½ cups wild rice, rinsed
4 ½ cups water
6 skinless, boneless chicken breast halves (about ½ pound each), rinsed and patted dry
6 ounces fontina cheese, cut into 6 equal strips
2 tablespoons butter
½ pound fresh shiitake mushrooms, cleaned, stems discarded, and caps thickly sliced (6 cups)
2 medium leeks, white parts only, well rinsed and chopped (1 cup)

12 oil-packed sun-dried tomatoes, drained and finely chopped (3 tablespoons)
3 large garlic cloves, minced
3 tablespoons minced fresh basil leaves or 1 tablespoon dried, crumbled
1 ½ tablespoons minced fresh thyme leaves or 1 ½ teaspoons dried, crumbled
6 slices bacon
¼ cup dry white wine
Chopped fresh parsley for garnish, optional

**PREP TIME:
50 MIN

BAKE TIME:
20–25 MIN**

1. In a medium saucepan, bring wild rice and water to a boil. Reduce heat, cover, and simmer until rice is almost tender, about 45 minutes. Drain well.
2. Meanwhile, place chicken breasts one at a time between 2 sheets of plastic wrap and, using the flat surface of a meat mallet or a rolling pin, pound to about ⅛-inch thickness. Lay a piece of fontina in middle of each chicken breast. Set aside.
3. Lightly butter a shallow 3-quart casserole. In a large skillet, melt butter over medium heat. Add mushrooms and leeks and sauté until vegetables are soft, about 5 minutes. Stir in rice. Transfer mixture to prepared casserole.
4. In a small bowl, mash together sun-dried tomatoes, garlic, basil, and thyme. Set aside.
5. Place 1 tablespoon (2 teaspoons if using dried herbs) of the sun-dried tomato mixture on each breast. Starting with a narrow end, roll up chicken to enclose filling. Repeat until all chicken breasts are stuffed.
6. Preheat oven to 425°F. In a large skillet, cook bacon for 3 minutes, until the fat is rendered. Remove to paper towels to drain briefly. Spiral-wrap each chicken bundle with one slice of partially cooked bacon. Place chicken bundles on top of rice.
7. Pour wine over casserole. Bake, uncovered, until chicken is no longer pink when tested with a knife (don't cut through to the filling), 20 to 25 minutes. If desired, garnish with chopped parsley just before serving.

1 serving: 679 calories, 69 g protein, 25 g total fat (11.8 g saturated), 42 g carbohydrates, 566 mg sodium, 185 mg cholesterol, 4 g dietary fiber

BARBECUED CHICKEN WITH JALAPEÑO JELLY

Jalapeño pepper jelly is popular throughout the Heartland. Most every regional community cookbook has one or more recipes for the spicy spread. Here the jelly flavors a barbecue sauce to go over chicken and onions for a mildly spicy casserole. If sweet onions (Vidalia, Maui, Texas 1015 Supersweet, or Walla Walla) are in season, by all means use them. You can always buy jalapeño jelly in your supermarket, but I've also given my favorite recipe here.

½ cup ketchup
⅓ cup mild vegetable oil, such as canola
3 tablespoons cider vinegar
3 tablespoons fresh lemon juice
   (1 large lemon)
1 small onion, preferably sweet,
   finely chopped (½ cup)
3 large garlic cloves, minced
2 tablespoons light brown sugar
2 tablespoons Worcestershire sauce

1 teaspoon dry mustard
1 teaspoon sweet paprika
   Salt, optional, and freshly ground black
   pepper to taste
⅓ cup jalapeño jelly (recipe follows)
1 whole chicken (3 to 3 ½ pounds),
   cut into quarters, skin discarded, rinsed,
   and patted dry
3 medium onions, preferably sweet,
   sliced (4 ½ cups)

PREP TIME:
25 MIN
BAKE TIME:
1 1/4 HR

1. Preheat oven to 375°F. In a medium saucepan, whisk together ketchup, oil, vinegar, lemon juice, chopped onion, garlic, brown sugar, Worcestershire sauce, mustard, paprika, salt, if desired, and pepper. Bring to a boil over medium-high heat and cook, whisking often, for 15 minutes. Remove from heat and whisk in jelly until well blended. Set aside.

2. Arrange chicken pieces in a shallow 3-quart casserole. Arrange onion slices over chicken. Pour sauce over onions and chicken.

3. Bake, uncovered, for 1 hour and 15 minutes, until chicken is tender and the juices run clear when chicken is pierced with a knife. Baste 2 or 3 times during baking with sauce. Serve right away.

1 serving: 552 calories, 39 g protein, 24 g total fat (2.7 g saturated), 47 g carbohydrates, 584 mg sodium, 119 mg cholesterol, 2 g dietary fiber

JALAPEÑO JELLY

MAKES 1 QUART

PREP TIME: 10 MINUTES · COOK TIME: 10 MIN + SEVERAL HOURS TO COOL

When handling jalapeños, use rubber gloves and immediately wash your hands with soap and hot water afterward to avoid any irritation to your hands or eyes.

½ large green or red bell pepper, seeded and finely chopped (¾ cup)

3 red or green jalapeño chile peppers, seeded and finely chopped (⅓ cup)

5 cups sugar

1 cup cider vinegar

2 3-ounce pouches liquid pectin

2 tablespoons fresh lemon juice

1. In a medium saucepan, mix bell pepper, chile peppers, sugar, and vinegar. Bring to a boil over medium-high heat, stirring constantly. Reduce heat and boil gently, stirring constantly, until sugar is dissolved, 5 to 7 minutes. Stir in pectin and boil for 1 minute, stirring constantly.

2. Remove from heat and skim off any foam. Stir in lemon juice.

3. Spoon mixture into hot sterilized half-pint canning jars to within ½ inch of top. Run a metal spatula or knife between jelly and jar to release any air bubbles. Wipe rims and threads with a damp clean cloth. Place dome lids on jars and tightly screw on ring bands. Cool jelly for several hours away from drafts on a towel. Test for a complete seal by pressing down on center of each lid with your finger. If the lids are down or stay down, they are sealed. Label and store in a cool, dry place. If jars are not completely sealed, refrigerate and use within 1 month.

1 tablespoon: 62 calories, 0 protein, 0 total fat (0 saturated), 16 g carbohydrates, 0 sodium, 0 cholesterol, 0 dietary fiber

INDIVIDUAL CHICKEN AND CORN TAMALE PIES

MAKES 4 SERVINGS

This is a contemporary and fresh-tasting version of tamale pie, using boneless chicken breasts instead of beef. Tomatillos resemble small green tomatoes wrapped in papery husks. They add a lemony herb flavor to the casserole. If your market doesn't carry fresh tomatillos, look for them in the Mexican canned goods section of large supermarkets. Serve the pies with an avocado and tomato salad. For dessert, peel and slice several tangerines and sprinkle with a little dark rum and confectioners' sugar.

CORNMEAL CRUST
5 ¼ cups low-sodium chicken broth
2 ¼ cups stone-ground yellow cornmeal
 1 teaspoon ground cumin
 ½ teaspoon salt
 ¼ teaspoon cayenne pepper

CHICKEN FILLING
 1 tablespoon olive oil
1 ½ pounds skinless, boneless chicken breasts, cut into 1-inch pieces
 1 cup fresh or thawed frozen corn kernels

 1 medium yellow onion, chopped (1 cup)
 1 medium tomato, chopped (1 cup)
 2 medium tomatillos, husked and chopped (⅔ cup)
 2 jalapeño chile peppers, seeded and minced (¼ cup)
 2 large garlic cloves, minced
 1 tablespoon chili powder
 ½ teaspoon ground cumin
 2 teaspoons fresh lemon juice
 1 cup shredded sharp Cheddar cheese (¼ pound)

PREP TIME: 45 MIN
BAKE TIME: 15–20 MIN
STAND TIME: 5 MIN

1. Preheat oven to 450°F. Generously butter four 15-ounce individual casseroles. Set aside.

2. **To make cornmeal crust:** In a large saucepan, bring chicken broth to a boil over medium-high heat. Stir in cornmeal, cumin, salt, and cayenne. Reduce heat to medium and cook, stirring constantly, until thickened, 10 to 12 minutes. Immediately spread mixture to a depth of about ½ inch over bottom and sides of prepared casseroles. Set aside.

3. **To make filling:** In a large skillet, heat oil over medium-high heat. Add chicken pieces and sauté until brown on all sides, about 5 minutes. Stir in corn, onion, tomato, tomatillos, jalapeños, garlic, chili powder, cumin, lemon juice, and cheese until blended. Spoon mixture into casseroles over cornmeal crusts.

4. Bake pies, uncovered, for 15 to 20 minutes, until crust is golden brown and filling is bubbly. Remove from oven and let stand on a wire rack for 5 minutes. Invert casseroles onto individual serving plates.

Advance Preparation: Casseroles may be made ahead through step 3, covered tightly, and refrigerated overnight or up to 24 hours. Bring to room temperature before baking.

1 serving: 722 calories, 58 g protein, 19 g total fat (7.9 g saturated), 79 g carbohydrates, 663 mg sodium, 130 mg cholesterol, 9 g dietary fiber

DEEP-DISH CHICKEN POTPIE

MAKES 6 SERVINGS

Once the last snow has melted and the lilacs and redbuds have burst into bloom, it's morel mushroom season in the northern woods of the Heartland. Available in produce markets from April through June, the cone-shaped mushrooms are also sold dried. Here morels add a distinctive, earthy flavor to this old-fashioned chicken potpie. If you prefer, you can substitute other wild mushrooms such as shiitake or porcini or cultivated white mushrooms. After a busy day at work, there's nothing more comforting than a potpie. Prepare it the night before so it's ready to pop into the oven when you get home. While the pie's baking, prepare a crisp salad and arrange a plate of fresh fruit and cheese for dessert.

PASTRY CRUST

- 1 ½ cups sifted unbleached all-purpose flour
- 1 tablespoon grated lemon rind
- ½ teaspoon salt
- ½ cup (1 stick) cold butter, cut into small pieces
- 3 to 4 tablespoons ice water

CHICKEN FILLING

- 1 tablespoon mild vegetable oil, such as canola
- 1 large yellow onion, chopped (1 ½ cups)
- 2 large garlic cloves, minced
- 2 medium celery ribs with leaves, chopped (1 ½ cups)
- 2 pounds skinless, boneless chicken breast halves, rinsed, patted dry, and cut crosswise into 1-inch-wide strips
- ¼ cup (½ stick) butter

- 5 tablespoons unbleached all-purpose flour
- 1 cup low-sodium chicken broth
- ¼ cup dry white wine
- ¼ pound fresh morels, cleaned and quartered, or 1 ounce dried morels, soaked in warm water for 45 minutes and drained, then quartered
- 2 medium carrots, peeled and sliced (1 ½ cups)
- 3 tablespoons minced fresh flat-leaf parsley
- 1 tablespoon minced fresh thyme leaves or 1 teaspoon dried, crumbled
- 1 teaspoon chopped fresh rosemary leaves or ¼ teaspoon dried, crumbled
- 2 medium zucchini, unpeeled, trimmed, and cut into ½-inch pieces (3 cups)
- ½ cup heavy cream
- 1 large egg, beaten with 1 tablespoon water

PREP TIME: 45 MIN

BAKE TIME: 25–30 MIN

1. **To make pastry by hand:** In a medium bowl, combine flour, lemon rind, and salt. Using a pastry blender or 2 knives, cut in butter until mixture resembles coarse crumbs. Drizzle with ice water, 1 tablespoon at a time, and stir with a fork after each addition until flour clumps together to form a dough.
   To make pastry in a food processor: Place flour, lemon rind, and salt in food processor and process for 1 second. Add butter and pulse on/off until mixture resembles coarse crumbs. With motor running, add water, 1 tablespoon at a time, through feed tube and process just until dough leaves side of bowl and forms a ball.
2. Gather dough into a ball and flatten into a disk. Wrap in plastic wrap and chill while preparing the filling.

3. To make filling: In a large skillet, heat oil over medium heat. Add onion and garlic and sauté until onion is soft, about 5 minutes. Add celery and sauté for another 3 minutes. Using a slotted spoon, remove mixture to a small bowl and set aside.

4. In same skillet, cook chicken over medium-high heat until browned on all sides, about 5 minutes. Using a slotted spoon, remove chicken to plate and set aside.

5. In same skillet, melt butter over medium heat. Stir in flour and cook, scraping the browned bits from bottom of pan, until mixture begins to foam. Stir in chicken broth, wine, morels, carrots, parsley, thyme, rosemary, and reserved onion-celery mixture. Cook, stirring occasionally, for 5 minutes. Stir in chicken, zucchini, and cream until blended. Remove from heat.

6. Preheat oven to 425°F. Pour chicken mixture into a deep 2-quart casserole or soufflé dish. On a lightly floured work surface, roll out and trim dough to shape of your casserole but 1 inch larger. Brush edge of dish with a little beaten egg. Place dough over filling, turn edges under, and crimp. Brush top of pastry with beaten egg. Cut a slit in center of pastry for steam to escape.

7. Place potpie on a baking sheet and bake, uncovered, until filling is heated through and crust is golden, 25 to 30 minutes. Serve right away.

Advance Preparation: Potpie may be made ahead through step 6, covered tightly, and refrigerated overnight or up to 24 hours. Bring to room temperature before baking.

1 serving: 677 calories, 44 g protein, 37 g total fat (20.1 g saturated), 42 g carbohydrates, 580 mg sodium, 213 mg cholesterol, 5 g dietary fiber

HARVEST GAME HEN CASSEROLE

MAKES 4 SERVINGS

Once an item found only in fancy restaurants, Cornish game hens are now readily available in supermarkets, either fresh or frozen, throughout the Heartland. Here they roast to perfection with a virtual cornucopia of vegetables ideal for cool-weather dining. For convenience, you can ask your butcher to split the hens for you. A whole head of garlic roasts with the hens and vegetables. The cloves will become very soft and the harsh garlic flavor will mellow. Squeeze the pulp out of the cloves to eat along with the meal.

2 Cornish game hens (about 1 ½ pounds each), split in half lengthwise
⅓ cup fresh lemon juice (2 small lemons)
1 tablespoon minced fresh thyme leaves or 1 teaspoon dried, crumbled
1 teaspoon minced fresh rosemary leaves or ¼ teaspoon dried, crumbled
2 large red-skinned potatoes, scrubbed and cut into ½-inch-thick slices (3 cups)
1 medium head garlic

2 small Japanese eggplants, unpeeled, trimmed, and cut diagonally into ½-inch-thick slices
4 plum tomatoes, quartered lengthwise
2 medium zucchini, trimmed and cut into ½-inch-thick slices (3 cups)
   Salt, optional, and freshly ground black pepper to taste
¼ cup olive oil

PREP TIME: 20 MIN + 1 HR TO MARINATE
BAKE TIME: 40–45 MIN

1. Rinse game hens and pat dry. Discard neck and giblets or reserve for another use. Remove and discard skin. Place hens in a large heavy-duty zipper-type plastic bag.

2. In a small bowl, mix lemon juice, thyme, and rosemary. Pour mixture into bag, seal, and refrigerate for 1 hour, turning bag frequently.

3. Preheat oven to 400°F. Lightly butter a shallow 4-quart casserole and set aside. Remove hens from marinade and pat dry. Discard marinade.

4. Slice ½ inch off top of garlic head. Place whole garlic head in center of prepared casserole. Arrange hens around garlic. Arrange vegetables around hens. Season hens and vegetables with salt, if desired, and pepper. Drizzle with oil.

5. Bake, uncovered, for 40 to 45 minutes, until thigh juices run clear when tested with a knife and vegetables are tender. Pour off excess oil and serve right away. Separate garlic head into individual cloves to squeeze onto hens and vegetables.

1 serving: 487 calories, 41 g protein, 23 g total fat (4.5 g saturated), 30 g carbohydrates, 80 mg sodium, 110 mg cholesterol, 5 g dietary fiber

BAKED LIMA BEAN AND CHICKEN DINNER

The idea for this recipe came from the wife of a farmer who grows lima beans for the Green Giant Company. We were speaking by phone about another subject entirely when she mentioned what she was putting in the oven as we talked. The dish sounded delicious—and it is. As the chicken bakes, make a salad and bake some apples or pears alongside the casserole for dessert.

4 chicken leg and thigh quarters (about 2 pounds), rinsed and patted dry
Salt, optional, and freshly ground black pepper to taste
2 tablespoons olive oil
1 medium onion, chopped (1 cup)
1 small red bell pepper, seeded and chopped (½ cup)
2 large garlic cloves, minced
1 10-ounce package frozen lima beans, thawed

1 16-ounce can stewed tomatoes
2 tablespoons chili powder
1 tablespoon Worcestershire sauce
¼ cup drained sliced pickled jalapeño chile peppers
½ cup shredded Monterey Jack cheese (2 ounces)
Chopped fresh cilantro leaves for garnish, optional
Sliced green onions for garnish, optional

PREP TIME: 30 MIN
BAKE TIME: 1 HR

1. Preheat oven to 350°F. Lightly butter a shallow 3-quart casserole. Season chicken pieces with salt, if desired, and pepper. Set aside.

2. In a large skillet, heat oil over medium heat. Add onion, bell pepper, and garlic and sauté until vegetables are soft, about 5 minutes. Add lima beans and cook, stirring often, for 1 minute. Using a slotted spoon, remove vegetable mixture to prepared casserole. Set aside.

3. In same skillet, add chicken pieces and cook over medium-high heat until browned, 6 to 8 minutes, turning once. Arrange chicken on top of vegetables.

4. In a medium bowl, combine tomatoes, chili powder, and Worcestershire sauce. Pour over chicken and vegetables.

5. Bake, covered, for 50 minutes or until chicken is tender and juices run clear when chicken is pierced with a knife. Uncover and sprinkle with pickled jalapeños and cheese. Bake, uncovered, for 10 minutes more, until cheese melts. Sprinkle with cilantro and green onions, if desired, and serve right away.

Advance Preparation: Casserole may be made ahead through step 4, covered tightly, and refrigerated overnight or up to 24 hours. Bring to room temperature before baking.

1 serving: 579 calories, 41 g protein, 33 g total fat (9.8 g saturated), 30 g carbohydrates, 797 mg sodium, 151 mg cholesterol, 9 g dietary fiber

PINEAPPLE CHICKEN

MAKES 4 SERVINGS

This unusual combination of pineapple and Cheddar cheese makes for a delightful chicken casserole. My mother used to make this yummy chicken dish using her home-canned pineapple slices, but I prefer using crushed pineapple—just be sure it's juice-packed or the dish will be overly sweet. Serve it with cooked white or brown rice that has been sautéed for 5 minutes in a little butter, minced onion, minced green bell pepper, and minced pimiento for a terrific midwinter dish that tastes of the tropics.

2 tablespoons butter, melted
2 shallots, minced (2 tablespoons)
1 16-ounce can juice-packed crushed pineapple, drained and juice reserved
1 whole chicken (3 to 3 ½ pounds), cut into serving pieces, skin discarded, rinsed, and patted dry

Salt, optional, and freshly ground black pepper to taste
3 tablespoons unbleached all-purpose flour
3 tablespoons packed light brown sugar
1 ½ cups shredded sharp Cheddar cheese (6 ounces)
1 tablespoon soy sauce

PREP TIME: 15 MIN

BAKE TIME: 1 HR

1. Preheat oven to 375°F. Brush bottom of a 13 x 9-inch baking dish with melted butter. Scatter shallots over bottom. Spoon half of crushed pineapple into dish and spread evenly with back of a spoon.

2. Arrange chicken pieces on top of pineapple. Season with salt, if desired, and pepper. Spoon remaining crushed pineapple over chicken.

3. In a small bowl, combine flour, brown sugar, and cheese. Sprinkle over casserole. In another small bowl, mix reserved pineapple juice and soy sauce. Pour over casserole.

4. Bake casserole, uncovered, for 1 hour, until chicken is tender and juices run clear when chicken is pierced with a knife.

1 serving: 545 calories, 48 g protein, 25 g total fat (13.9 g saturated), 31 g carbohydrates, 714 mg sodium, 179 mg cholesterol, 1 g dietary fiber

TURKEY AND ARTICHOKE CASSEROLE

MAKES 6 SERVINGS

The contrasting flavors and textures of pasta, turkey, and artichoke hearts, bound in a silky sherry-favored sauce, make this casserole special. So special it's a good reason to roast a turkey often, just for the leftovers. Serve it for Sunday brunch with a basket of toasted English muffins.

½ pound dried rotini (corkscrew-shaped) pasta
2 9-ounce packages frozen artichoke hearts
¼ cup (½ stick) butter
½ pound fresh mushrooms, cleaned, trimmed, and sliced (3 cups)
3 tablespoons finely chopped white onion
5 tablespoons unbleached all-purpose flour
3 cups evaporated milk

3 tablespoons minced fresh flat-leaf parsley
¼ cup dry sherry
Salt, optional, and freshly ground black pepper to taste
6 cups chopped cooked turkey
1 ½ cups shredded Swiss cheese (6 ounces)
Sweet paprika for garnish, optional

PREP TIME: 35 MIN
BAKE TIME: 25–30 MIN

1. Preheat oven to 350°F. Lightly butter a shallow 4-quart casserole and set aside.
2. Cook pasta according to package directions. Drain well and set aside.
3. Cook artichoke hearts according to package directions. Drain well and set aside.
4. Meanwhile, in a large saucepan, melt 2 tablespoons butter over medium heat. Add mushrooms and onion and sauté until vegetables are soft, about 5 minutes. Using a slotted spoon, remove vegetables to a plate and set aside.
5. In same saucepan, melt remaining 2 tablespoons butter. Stir flour into butter. Reduce heat to low and cook, stirring constantly, until flour is golden, about 2 minutes.
6. Whisk in evaporated milk. Increase heat to medium and cook, stirring constantly, until mixture just comes to a boil. Remove from heat and stir in mushroom mixture, parsley, sherry, salt, if desired, and pepper. Transfer mixture to a large bowl.
7. Gently stir in artichoke hearts, pasta, and turkey. Transfer to prepared casserole. Sprinkle with cheese and dust lightly with paprika, if desired.
8. Bake casserole, uncovered, for 25 to 30 minutes, until cheese is melted and mixture is bubbly. Serve right away.

1 serving: 781 calories, 66 g protein, 33 g total fat (17.8 g saturated), 54 g carbohydrates, 426 mg sodium, 189 mg cholesterol, 5 g dietary fiber

CURRIED TURKEY CASSEROLE

MAKES 4 SERVINGS

Health-conscious cooks throughout the Heartland are replacing ground beef with ground turkey, which is now available in practically every supermarket, to lower their calorie and fat intake. Here ground turkey stars in an easy make-ahead-and-bake-later casserole that's especially welcome after a hard day of work or shopping. The casserole has a flavor similar to Indian curries, a taste introduced to the Midwest by students from India who came to Heartland state universities to study home economics and agriculture. To serve, add a fresh fruit salad, sprinkled with orange juice and chopped mint.

½   pound dried rigatoni or ziti pasta
1   tablespoon olive oil
1   large yellow onion, chopped
    (1 ½ cups)
2   large garlic cloves, minced
1 ½ pounds ground turkey
1   14 ½-ounce can stewed tomatoes
1   10 ¾-ounce reduced-fat condensed cream
    of chicken soup
1   cup frozen whole-kernel corn, thawed

1   tablespoon Worcestershire sauce
1   tablespoon curry powder or to taste
¼   teaspoon cayenne pepper
¼   teaspoon ground cumin
¼   teaspoon ground ginger
⅛   teaspoon ground turmeric
    Salt, optional, and freshly ground pepper
    to taste
    Chopped fresh cilantro or parsley for garnish,
    optional

**PREP TIME:
30 MIN
BAKE TIME:
30-35 MIN**

1. Preheat oven to 350°F. Lightly butter a shallow 3-quart casserole. Set aside.
2. Cook pasta according to package directions. Drain well and set aside.
3. Meanwhile, in a large skillet, heat oil over medium heat. Add onion and garlic and sauté until onion is soft, about 5 minutes. Add turkey and cook, breaking up meat with a wooden spoon, for about 10 minutes, until no longer pink. Using a slotted spoon, remove mixture to a large bowl.
4. Add pasta, tomatoes, soup, corn, Worcestershire sauce, curry powder, cayenne, cumin, ginger, turmeric, salt, if desired, and pepper and stir until well blended. Transfer mixture to prepared casserole.
5. Bake casserole, uncovered, for 30 to 35 minutes, until bubbly. If desired, garnish with chopped cilantro before serving.

Advance Preparation: Casserole may be made ahead through step 4, covered tightly, and refrigerated overnight or up to 24 hours. Bring to room temperature before baking.

1 serving: 631 calories, 41 g protein, 24 g total fat (6.0 g saturated), 66 g carbohydrates, 674 mg sodium, 143 mg cholesterol, 5 g dietary fiber

ENCHILADA CASSEROLE

MAKES 4 SERVINGS

Tex-Mex food has always been popular in the Midwest. It's even likely that early settlers were first introduced to it in the late 1800s by the trail drives out of Texas that passed through the Plains. Nowadays, with an increased interest in spicy foods and the influx of immigrants from Mexico throughout the Heartland, once-hard-to-find items such as fresh tortillas, fresh chile peppers, and cilantro are readily available in most supermarkets.

1 ½ pounds ground turkey
1 large green bell pepper, seeded and chopped (1 cup)
1 medium yellow onion, chopped (1 cup)
1 jalapeño chile pepper, seeded and minced (2 tablespoons)
1 large garlic clove, minced
1 14 ½-ounce can stewed tomatoes
1 1 ½-ounce package taco seasoning mix
½ cup water

2 tablespoons mild vegetable oil, such as canola
8 9-inch corn tortillas
½ cup shredded Cheddar cheese (2 ounces)
2 10-ounce cans mild or hot enchilada sauce
½ cup sour cream
1 cup shredded Monterey Jack cheese (¼ pound)
6 pitted black olives, sliced (⅓ cup), optional

PREP TIME: 35 MIN

BAKE TIME: 35–40 MIN

1. Preheat oven to 350°F. Lightly grease a 13 x 9-inch baking dish and set aside.
2. In a large nonstick skillet, cook ground turkey over medium-high heat, breaking up meat with a wooden spoon, for about 5 minutes, until no longer pink. Drain off all fat. Add bell pepper, onion, jalapeño, and garlic and cook, stirring frequently, for 5 minutes. Stir in tomatoes, seasoning mix, and water. Continue to cook another 5 minutes, stirring often. Remove from heat and set aside.
3. In another large skillet, heat oil over medium-high heat. Add tortillas, one at a time, and cook for 5 to 10 seconds, until soft. Drain on paper towels.
4. Spoon ¼ cup of pork mixture into center of a tortilla and sprinkle with 1 tablespoon Cheddar cheese. Roll up and place seam-side down in prepared baking dish. Repeat procedure until all tortillas are filled.
5. Stir enchilada sauce into remaining turkey mixture and spoon over filled tortillas.
6. Bake casserole, covered, for 25 minutes. Uncover and spread with sour cream. Sprinkle with Monterey Jack cheese and black olives, if desired. Bake, uncovered, for 10 to 15 minutes more, until cheese is melted. Serve right away.

Advance Preparation: Casserole may be made ahead through step 5, covered tightly, and refrigerated overnight or up to 24 hours. Bring to room temperature before baking.

1 serving: 730 calories, 38 g protein, 39 g total fat (15.4 g saturated), 58 g carbohydrates, 2,052 mg sodium, 135 mg cholesterol, 5 g dietary fiber

CHIPPED BEEF CASSEROLE

Wafer-thin slices of smoked, dried beef (chipped beef) became a Midwestern household staple during the Depression, when beef and other scarce food items were rationed. When the rationing stopped, chipped beef was still frequently served at our house since my mother was a thrifty shopper and cook. I learned to make chipped beef on toast and chipped beef casserole in my first cooking class in junior high. This version is quite tasty—it's a good, hearty casserole to serve after an afternoon of hiking.

½ pound dried farfalle (bow-tie-shaped) pasta
1 pound fresh asparagus spears
   or 1 10-ounce package frozen chopped
   asparagus
3 2½-ounce packages sliced smoked beef,
   torn into bite-size pieces
2 10¾-ounce cans condensed cream of
   mushroom soup

2 cups whole milk
1 medium yellow onion, chopped (1 cup)
1 large garlic clove, minced
1 medium red bell pepper, seeded and
   chopped (1 cup)
4 hard-cooked large eggs, peeled and sliced
1 cup shredded sharp Cheddar cheese
   (¼ pound)

PREP TIME: 20 MIN
BAKE TIME: 1 HR

1. Preheat oven to 350°F. Lightly butter a shallow 3-quart casserole and set aside.
2. Cook pasta according to package directions. Drain well and set aside.
3. Meanwhile, snap off and discard tough stem ends of fresh asparagus. Cut asparagus spears diagonally into 1½-inch pieces. Blanch in boiling water until crisp-tender, about 4 minutes. Drain well. (If using frozen asparagus, blanch for 1 minute.) Arrange asparagus over bottom of prepared casserole.
4. In a large bowl, mix beef, pasta, soup, milk, onion, garlic, and bell pepper. Spoon half of beef mixture evenly over asparagus in casserole. Cover with egg slices. Spread remaining beef mixture over eggs and cover with cheese.
5. Bake casserole, uncovered, for 1 hour, until heated through and bubbly. Serve right away.

1 serving: 503 calories, 27 g protein, 23 g total fat (9.9 g saturated), 47 g carbohydrates, 1,537 mg sodium, 199 mg cholesterol, 4 g dietary fiber

KLAUSENBERGER

MAKES 6 SERVINGS

Sue Steinman, my son's mother-in-law, grew up on a farm in southern Ohio. One of six children, she spent a lot of her time helping her mother, Elsie Burkle, prepare the meals for the family and farmhands. This was a frequently made casserole, sturdy enough to appease hungry appetites after a day of plowing or haying. It is named after the town of Klausenberg in Transylvania, where the dish originated.

1 tablespoon mild vegetable oil, such as canola
1 pound lean ground beef
1 pound ground pork
1 large yellow onion, chopped (1 ½ cups)
1 cup long-grain white rice

Salt, optional, and freshly ground black pepper to taste
1 32-ounce jar sauerkraut, well drained
2 cups water
2 large eggs
2 tablespoons unbleached all-purpose flour
2 tablespoons sour cream

PREP TIME: 20 MIN
BAKE TIME: 1 1/4 HR

1. Preheat oven to 350°F. Lightly butter a 13 x 9-inch baking dish and set aside.

2. In a large nonstick skillet, cook beef and pork over medium-high heat, breaking up meat with a wooden spoon, for about 5 minutes, until no longer pink. Drain off all fat. Stir in onion and rice. Season with salt, if desired, and pepper. Set aside.

3. Place one-third of drained sauerkraut over bottom of prepared casserole. Top with half of meat mixture. Spread another third of the sauerkraut over the meat; top with remaining meat mixture, then remaining sauerkraut. Pour water evenly over casserole.

4. Bake casserole, uncovered, for 1 hour. In a small bowl, whisk eggs until frothy. Whisk in flour and sour cream until well blended. Uncover casserole and spoon egg mixture evenly over casserole. Bake, uncovered, until top is golden brown, about 15 minutes more. Serve right away.

Advance Preparation: Casserole may be made ahead through step 3, covered tightly, and refrigerated overnight or up to 24 hours. Bring to room temperature before baking.

1 serving: 511 calories, 33 g protein, 26 g total fat (9.1 g saturated), 34 g carbohydrates, 805 mg sodium, 172 mg cholesterol, 4 g dietary fiber

END-OF-THE-MONTH POTPIE

MAKES 4 SERVINGS

This is a great budget stretcher casserole—the type of hearty casserole I'd fix when my husband, David, and I were first married and living on a tight budget, saving to buy our first house. I still make this dish during the winter when the children come home for visits and there's a hungry crowd for lunch. It can easily be doubled or tripled.

PASTRY CRUST

1 ¼	cups unbleached all-purpose flour
¼	teaspoon salt
⅓	cup (5 ⅓ tablespoons) cold butter, cut into small pieces
1	large egg
2	to 3 tablespoons ice water

MEAT FILLING

½	pound lean ground beef
½	pound ground pork
1	large yellow onion, chopped (1 ½ cups)
2	medium celery ribs, chopped (1 cup)
1	medium green bell pepper, seeded and chopped (1 cup)
2	large garlic cloves, minced
1	14 ½-ounce can plum tomatoes, chopped, undrained
1	4-ounce can sliced mushrooms, drained
1 ½	teaspooons Worcestershire sauce
¼	cup finely chopped fresh flat-leaf parsley
¼	teaspoon hot pepper sauce or to taste
	Salt, optional, and freshly ground black pepper to taste
1	cup shredded Cheddar cheese (¼ pound)

PREP TIME: 45 MIN
BAKE TIME: 30–35 MIN

1. **To make pastry by hand:** In a medium bowl, combine flour and salt. Usin_ _astry blender or two knives, cut in butter until mixture resembles coarse crum___ a small bowl, whisk egg until frothy. Whisk in 1 tablespoon ice water. Spr___ _e mixture over the crumbs and toss with a fork. If needed, sprinkle with 1 or 2 ___itional tablespoons ice water and toss with a fork until mixture clumps togeth___ _ form a dough. Gather the dough into a ball.

To make pastry in a food processor: Put flour and sa__ _ood processor and process for 1 second. Add butter and pulse on/off until mixture r___les coarse crumbs. In a small bowl, whisk egg until frothy. With motor running, add egg mixture ___ugh feed tube. Add 1 tablespoon ice water and process just until dough leaves side of bowl and for__ _ball, adding 1 or 2 additional tablespoons ice water if needed.

2. Form the pastry into a flat disk and wrap in pl___ _wrap. Refrigerate for at least 30 minutes.

3. Meanwhile, preheat oven to 350°F. Light__ __tter a shallow 2-quart casserole. In a large nonstick skillet, cook beef and pork over medium-high h__ __reaking up meat with a wooden spoon, for about 5 minutes, until no longer pink. Drain off all fat. __ _nion, celery, bell pepper, and garlic and cook, stirring frequently, for 5 minutes.

4. Add tomatoes, mushroo___, Worcestershire sauce, parsley, hot pepper sauce, salt, if desired, and pepper. Stir in cheese. Spoon m__t mixture into prepared casserole. Set aside.

5. On a lightly flo___d work surface, roll out dough ¼ inch thick and trim to shape of your casserole but 1 inch larger. Pl__e dough over filling, turn edges under, and crimp. Using a sharp knife, cut 2 or 3 small decorative ve___ in dough to allow steam to escape.

6. Set potpie on a baking sheet and bake, uncovered, until pastry is lightly browned and filling is bubbling, about 30 to 35 minutes. Serve right away.

Advance Preparation: Casserole may be made ahead through step 5, covered, and refrigerated overnight or up to 24 hours. Bring to room temperature before baking.

1 serving: 703 calories, 37 g protein, 42 g total fat (21.9 g saturated), 45 g carbohydrates, 884 mg sodium, 199 mg cholesterol, 5 g dietary fiber

GRANDMA'S BEEF AND SPINACH BAKE

MAKES 4 SERVINGS

My mother used to make a similar dish that my sons dubbed "Grandma Meat." Even as youngsters, they loved spinach; but if it's not your family's favorite vegetable, you can substitute frozen chopped broccoli with good results.

¼ cup dry unseasoned bread crumbs
1 pound extra-lean ground beef
1 medium yellow onion, finely chopped (1 cup)
2 large garlic cloves, minced
1 10-ounce package frozen chopped spinach, thawed
1½ teaspoons chopped fresh basil leaves or ½ teaspoon dried, crumbled
1½ teaspoons chopped fresh oregano leaves or ½ teaspoon dried, crumbled
1 teaspoon chopped fresh marjoram leaves or ¼ teaspoon dried, crumbled

½ teaspoon chopped fresh rosemary leaves or ⅛ teaspoon dried, crumbled
2 tablespoons butter
3 tablespoons unbleached all-purpose flour
¾ cup whole milk
5 large eggs, separated
½ cup sour cream
1½ cups shredded Swiss cheese (6 ounces)
Salt, optional, and freshly ground black pepper to taste

PREP TIME: 40 MIN
BAKE TIME: 25–30 MIN

1. Preheat oven to 375°F. Lightly butter a deep 3-quart casserole and dust with 2 tablespoons bread crumbs. Set aside.

2. In a large nonstick skillet, cook beef, onion, and garlic over medium heat until meat is no longer pink, about 10 minutes. Drain off all fat. Stir in spinach and cook, stirring frequently, until liquid from spinach is absorbed, about 5 minutes. Stir in herbs.

3. In a large saucepan, melt butter over medium-high heat. Stir in flour. Add milk and cook, whisking constantly, until mixture is thickened, about 1 minute. Remove from heat and whisk in egg yolks, one at a time, until well blended. Whisk in sour cream, half of cheese, salt, if desired, and pepper. Stir in beef mixture.

4. In a medium bowl, using an electric mixer or a whisk, beat egg whites until stiff peaks form. Stir one-third of beaten egg whites into spinach mixture to lighten it. Using a rubber spatula, gently and thoroughly fold in remaining egg whites.

5. Transfer mixture to prepared casserole. Sprinkle with remaining cheese and remaining bread crumbs. Bake, uncovered, for 25 to 30 minutes, until puffed and center is softly set when casserole is shaken gently. Serve right away.

1 serving: 657 calories, 47 g protein, 43 g total fat (22.0 g saturated), 21 g carbohydrates, 442 mg sodium, 406 mg cholesterol, 3 g dietary fiber

TACO SALAD CASSEROLE

MAKES 6 SERVINGS

Taco salad is available throughout the Heartland in Tex-Mex restaurants, roadside cafés, and country diners. This hearty casserole, brimming with Mexican flavor, is sure to be a hit with everyone. If you're watching fat grams, substitute ground turkey for the ground beef and use reduced fat sour cream and cheese. Complete the meal with plenty of extra tortilla chips. Offer slices of melon for dessert.

2 pounds extra-lean ground beef

2 medium yellow onions, finely chopped (2 cups)

4 large garlic cloves, minced

2 15-ounce cans pinto beans, undrained

2 10-ounce cans diced tomatoes with green chiles

2 teaspoons chili powder

1 teaspoon ground cumin

1 teaspoon dried oregano leaves, crumbled

¾ cup sour cream

Salt, optional, and freshly ground black pepper to taste

¾ cup shredded sharp Cheddar cheese (3 ounces)

¾ cup shredded Monterey Jack cheese (3 ounces)

1 cup coarsely crumbled unsalted tortilla chips

1 medium head iceberg lettuce, shredded (6 cups)

Additional sour cream for garnish, optional

Medium or hot salsa for garnish, optional

PREP TIME: 20 MIN

BAKE TIME: 30–35 MIN

1. Preheat oven to 375°F. In a large nonstick skillet, cook beef over medium-high heat, breaking up meat with a wooden spoon, for about 5 minutes, until no longer pink. Drain off all fat. Add onion and garlic and cook, stirring frequently, for 5 minutes.

2. Stir in beans, tomatoes, chili powder, cumin, oregano, and sour cream. Taste and season with salt, if desired, and pepper. Transfer mixture to a shallow 4-quart casserole.

3. In a medium bowl, combine cheeses and tortilla chips. Sprinkle over casserole. Bake, uncovered, for 30 to 35 minutes, until mixture is heated through and bubbly and cheese is melted.

4. To serve, arrange 1 cup of shredded lettuce over each of 6 serving plates. Spoon hot casserole onto lettuce. Serve sour cream and salsa separately to spoon over each serving as desired.

Advance Preparation: Casserole may be made ahead through step 2, covered tightly, and refrigerated overnight or up to 24 hours. Bring to room temperature before topping and baking.

1 serving: 644 calories, 46 g protein, 34 g total fat (16.0 g saturated), 39 g carbohydrates, 1,249 mg sodium, 134 mg cholesterol, 8 g dietary fiber

PASTA SKILLET CASSEROLE

MAKES 4 SERVINGS

This recipe comes from my dear friend, Bonnie Sanders Polin, an excellent cook living in Tulsa, Oklahoma. Bonnie used to make this pasta pizza for her children, filling it with pepperoni, Italian sausage, leftover chicken, Canadian bacon, etc. Now that she and her husband, Jerry, are empty-nesters and cutting down on fat, she makes this healthier, still quite delicious, version.

PIZZA SAUCE

- ½ pound lean ground beef
- 1 large garlic clove, minced
- 2 green onions, white part and 1 inch green tops, thinly sliced (¼ cup)
- 1 28-ounce can Italian-style whole tomatoes, drained
- 1 ½ teaspoons chopped fresh basil leaves or ½ teaspoon dried, crumbled
- 1 teaspoon chopped fresh oregano leaves or ¼ teaspoon dried, crumbled
- ¼ teaspoon crushed red pepper
- ¼ teaspoon salt
- ¼ teaspoon sugar

PASTA CRUST

- ¼ pound dried thin spaghetti such as angel hair or capellini
- 1 tablespoon olive oil

TOPPINGS

- 1 small green bell pepper, seeded and thinly sliced into rings (¾ cup)
- ¼ pound fresh mushrooms, cleaned, trimmed, and thinly sliced (1 ½ cups)
- 1 cup shredded mozzarella cheese (¼ pound)
- 3 tablespoons freshly grated Parmesan cheese

PREP TIME: 1 HR
BAKE TIME: 15 MIN
STAND TIME: 5 MIN

1. **To make sauce:** In a large nonstick skillet, cook beef over medium-high heat, breaking it up with a wooden spoon, for about 5 minutes, until no longer pink. Drain off all fat. Stir in garlic and green onion and cook, stirring frequently, for 3 minutes.

2. Stir in tomatoes, crushing them with the back of a wooden spoon. Stir in herbs, red pepper, salt, if desired, and sugar. Reduce heat to medium-low and simmer, uncovered, until slightly thickened, about 15 minutes.

3. **Meanwhile, make pasta crust:** Cook pasta according to package directions. Drain well.

4. Preheat oven to 350°F. In a 10-inch nonstick ovenproof skillet, heat oil over medium heat. Add mushrooms and bell pepper and sauté until slightly softened, about 3 minutes. Remove vegetables to a plate.

5. In same skillet, evenly distribute cooked pasta, pressing down lightly with a spoon. Cover and cook over medium heat until pasta forms a crust, about 20 minutes.

6. To turn crust over, place a nonstick baking sheet over skillet and invert pasta onto it. Slide pasta back into skillet, tranfer to oven, and bake, uncovered, for 10 minutes.

7. Evenly spread sauce over pasta, leaving a thin border around edges. Top with bell pepper rings, mushrooms, and mozzarella cheese. Sprinkle with Parmesan cheese. Bake for 5 minutes more, until cheese is melted. Let stand for 5 minutes before cutting into wedges to serve.

1 serving: 389 calories, 25 g protein, 17 g total fat (7.0 g saturated), 34 g carbohydrates, 651 mg sodium, 57 mg cholesterol, 2 g dietary fiber

FARMER'S MEAT AND VEGETABLE BAKE

MAKES 4 SERVINGS

This has been a favorite at our house for years, the kind of recipe that changes as the children grow and their palates develop to appreciate new and stronger flavors. This is the way that I make it now that everyone's fond of spicier foods.

1   pound lean ground beef
½   pound ground pork
1   large yellow onion, chopped (1 ½ cups)
1   medium red bell pepper, seeded and chopped (1 cup)
1   jalapeño chile pepper, seeded and minced
2   large garlic cloves, minced
½   pound green cabbage, shredded (2 cups)
1   8-ounce can tomato sauce

¼   cup minced fresh cilantro
1   large russet potato, peeled and thinly sliced (1 ½ cups)
    Salt, optional, and freshly ground black pepper to taste
    Cayenne pepper to taste
1   cup shredded Monterey Jack cheese (¼ pound)
2   medium tomatoes, sliced

PREP TIME: 35 MIN
BAKE TIME: 45–50 MIN
STAND TIME: 5 MIN

1. Preheat oven to 375°F. Lightly butter a shallow 3-quart casserole and set aside.
2. In a large nonstick skillet, cook beef and pork over medium-high heat, breaking up meat with a wooden spoon, for about 5 minutes, until no longer pink. Drain off all fat. Add onion, bell pepper, jalapeño, and garlic and cook, stirring frequently, for 5 minutes more.
3. Lay cabbage over meat mixture in skillet. Reduce heat to low, cover, and cook until cabbage wilts, about 5 minutes. Stir in tomato sauce and cilantro. Remove from heat and set aside.
4. Line bottom of prepared casserole with potato slices, overlapping slightly to completely cover the surface. Season with salt, if desired, black pepper, and cayenne. Spoon meat mixture evenly over potatoes. Sprinkle with cheese and arrange tomato slices on top.
5. Bake casserole, uncovered, until mixture is bubbly and cheese is melted, 45 to 50 minutes. Remove from oven and let stand for 5 minutes before serving.

Advance Preparation: Casserole may be made ahead through step 4, covered tightly, and refrigerated overnight or up to 24 hours. Bring to room temperature before baking.

1 serving: 561 calories, 43 g protein, 31 g total fat (14.0 g saturated), 28 g carbohydrates, 613 mg sodium, 136 mg cholesterol, 5 g dietary fiber

COUNTRY LAMB WITH WHITE BEANS

MAKES 4 SERVINGS

I once took a class in open-hearth cooking. The instructor emphasized the need for pioneer women to "make do" during the long winter months, using the stores from the root cellar with only the contents of their spice cabinet to add variety. She went on to make a savory dried-meat stew, sweetened with cinnamon and allspice. When I decided to do a ground lamb casserole, I thought of that wonderful stew and came up with this recipe, using celery root and some spices that might have been on hand. Rather than cooking the navy beans from scratch, however, I opted to be modern and open a can.

1 tablespoon olive oil	¾ cup low-sodium chicken broth
1 medium yellow onion, chopped (1 cup)	1 tablespoon fresh lemon juice
2 large garlic cloves, minced	1 teaspoon ground allspice
1 small celery root, trimmed, peeled, and diced (1 cup)	½ teaspoon ground cinnamon
1½ pounds ground lamb	½ teaspoon ground ginger
1 15-ounce can navy beans, drained and rinsed	2 tablespoons minced fresh parsley for garnish, optional

**PREP TIME:
35 MIN**

**BAKE TIME:
35–45 MIN**

1. Preheat oven to 350°F. Lightly butter a deep 2-quart casserole and set aside.
2. In a large skillet, heat oil over medium heat. Add onion and garlic and sauté until onion is soft, about 5 minutes. Add celery root and sauté for 5 minutes. Using a slotted spoon, remove vegetables to a bowl and keep warm.
3. Add lamb to skillet and cook until no longer pink, breaking up meat with a wooden spoon, about 10 minutes. Drain off all fat.
4. Return vegetables to skillet. Stir in beans, broth, lemon juice, allspice, cinnamon, and ginger. Transfer mixture to prepared casserole.
5. Bake casserole, covered, until hot and bubbly, about 35 to 45 minutes. Garnish with chopped parsley, if desired. and serve right away.

Advance Preparation: Casserole may be made ahead through step 4, covered tightly, and refrigerated overnight or up to 24 hours. Bring to room temperature before baking.

1 serving: 483 calories, 36 g protein, 27 g total fat (10.1 g saturated), 24 g carbohydrates, 486 mg sodium, 112 mg cholesterol, 7 g dietary fiber

PORK AND DRIED FRUIT RAGOUT

MAKES 6 SERVINGS

Although hogs have been raised in the Heartland since the first settlers arrived there, it wasn't until 1954 that the farmers established the National Pork Producers Council, headquartered in Des Moines, Iowa. Of the ten states leading in pork production, nine are in the Heartland. Serve this hearty dish over pasta for a comforting Sunday night meal. Dried cherries are available in most large supermarkets and by mail order (see Sources, page 142). However, if you cannot find them, you could use golden raisins instead.

- 3 pounds boneless pork loin, cut into 1-inch cubes
- 24 dried apricot halves
- 1 cup dried cherries
- ½ cup bourbon
- ½ cup apricot nectar
- 2 shallots, minced (¼ cup)
- 1 tablespoon chopped fresh rosemary leaves or 1 teaspoon dried, crumbled

- 1 tablespoon chopped fresh sage leaves or 1 teaspoon dried, crumbled
- 2 tablespoons olive oil
- 1 cup dry white wine
- 3 cups low-sodium chicken broth
- 1 10-ounce package peeled baby carrots
- ½ pound frozen pearl onions (1 ¾ cups)

PREP TIME: 30 MIN + AT LEAST 4 HR TO MARINATE

BAKE TIME: 2 HR

1. In a large zipper-type plastic bag, combine pork, apricots, cherries, bourbon, nectar, shallots, rosemary, and sage. Seal bag and refrigerate at least 4 hours or overnight, turning bag occasionally.

2. Using a slotted spoon, remove meat from marinade to a medium bowl and remove dried fruit to a small bowl. Reserve marinade.

3. Preheat oven to 350°F. Pat pork dry. In a large skillet, heat oil over medium-high heat. Add pork and cook, stirring frequently, until browned, about 10 minutes. Using a slotted spoon, remove pork to a deep 3-quart casserole. Add reserved dried fruits to casserole.

4. Drain off any oil in skillet. Add reserved marinade and bring to a boil over medium-high heat. Cook, stirring to scrape up any browned bits from bottom of pan, for 5 minutes. Add wine, broth, carrots, and onions and return to a boil. Pour mixture over casserole.

5. Bake casserole, covered, for 1 ¼ hours. Uncover and bake for 45 minutes, until pork is tender. Serve right away.

Advance Preparation: Casserole may be made ahead through step 4, covered tightly, and refrigerated overnight or up to 24 hours. Bring to room temperature before baking.

1 serving: 610 calories, 52 g protein, 22 g total fat (6.8 g saturated), 37 g carbohydrates, 156 mg sodium, 138 mg cholesterol, 4 g dietary fiber

GARLICKY PORK CHOPS WITH ONIONS AND POTATOES

MAKES 4 SERVINGS

Iowa is one of the country's leading pork-producing states. This savory one-dish meal calls for Iowa chops, a lean he-man loin or rib pork chop that is cut 1 ¼ inches to 1 ½ inches thick. Coated with garlicky crumbs and pungent with herbs, the chops bake in a shallow casserole along with small whole onions and potatoes. The simple combination results in a dish suitable for company.

3 tablespoons olive oil
1 tablespoon butter
3 large garlic cloves, minced
½ cup dry unseasoned bread crumbs
1 teaspoon chopped fresh thyme leaves
  or ¼ teaspoon dried, crumbled
1 teaspoon chopped fresh sage leaves
  or ¼ teaspoon dried, crumbled
2 tablespoons finely chopped celery leaves

4 Iowa-cut pork chops
  (about 10 ounces each)
  Salt, optional, and freshly ground black
  pepper to taste
8 small white onions, peeled
8 tiny white new potatoes (about 1 ½ inches
  in diameter), scrubbed
  Chopped fresh parsley for garnish,
  optional

PREP TIME: 25 MIN
BAKE TIME: 45 MIN

1. Preheat oven to 400°F. Lightly grease a shallow 3-quart casserole and set aside.

2. In a medium skillet, heat 1 tablespoon oil and the butter over medium-low heat. Add garlic and sauté until fragrant, about 3 minutes. Add bread crumbs, thyme, sage, and celery leaves. Stir until crumbs are evenly moistened. Remove from heat.

3. Season pork chops with salt, if desired, and pepper. Press the bread crumb mixture onto both sides of the pork chops.

4. Arrange breaded pork chops in prepared casserole and surround with onions and potatoes. Drizzle with remaining 2 tablespoons olive oil.

5. Bake, uncovered, for 30 minutes. Turn vegetables and bake for 15 minutes more, until vegetables are tender and pork is done. Garnish with chopped parsley, if desired, and serve right away.

1 serving: 704 calories, 49 g protein, 42 g total fat (13.0 g saturated), 31 g carbohydrates, 257 mg sodium, 147 mg cholesterol, 4 g dietary fiber

PORK CHOP CASSEROLE WITH CABBAGE AND APPLES

MAKES 6 SERVINGS

Pork seems to have an affinity for apples. Here the two are baked on a bed of red cabbage, showing the German influence prevalent in the northern regions of the Heartland.

1 tablespoon mild vegetable oil, such as canola

6 center-cut bone-in pork chops, cut about 1 inch thick, well trimmed
Salt, optional, and freshly ground black pepper to taste

4 slices bacon

1 medium yellow onion, chopped (1 cup)

2 medium celery ribs with leaves, chopped (1 ½ cups)

2 large garlic cloves, minced

1 medium red cabbage (about 2 pounds), cored and thinly sliced (8 cups)

2 tart apples such as Granny Smith, Cortland, or Paula Red, peeled, cored, and diced (2 cups)

½ cup golden raisins

2 tablespoons light brown sugar

2 tablespoons fresh lemon juice

1 cup low-sodium chicken broth

½ cup dry red wine or additional broth

1 ½ teaspoons minced fresh thyme leaves or ½ teaspoon dried, crumbled

1 teaspoon minced fresh sage leaves or ¼ teaspoon dried, crumbled
Fresh thyme leaves for garnish, optional

PREP TIME: 55 MIN
BAKE TIME: 1–1 1/4 HR

1. Preheat oven to 350°F. Lightly grease a 13 x 9-inch baking dish. Set aside.

2. In a large skillet, heat oil over medium-high heat. Season pork chops with salt, if desired, and pepper. Add to skillet and brown for 3 minutes per side. Remove chops and set aside.

3. In same skillet, cook bacon over medium heat until crisp. Remove to paper towels to drain. Set aside.

4. Pour off all but 2 tablespoons of bacon drippings. Add onion, celery, and garlic to skillet and sauté over medium heat until vegetables are soft, about 5 minutes. Add cabbage and cook, stirring gently, for 5 minutes.

5. Remove from heat and stir in apples, raisins, brown sugar, and lemon juice. Spoon mixture into prepared baking dish. Arrange pork chops over cabbage mixture.

6. In a medium bowl, mix broth, wine, thyme, and sage. Pour over casserole.

7. Bake, covered, for 1 to 1 ¼ hours, until pork chops and cabbage are tender. Crumble reserved bacon and sprinkle over casserole. Garnish with fresh thyme leaves, if desired, and serve right away.

1 serving: 400 calories, 33 g protein, 16 g total fat (5.4 g saturated), 29 g carbohydrates, 235 mg sodium, 90 mg cholesterol, 4 g dietary fiber

PORK-STUFFED ONIONS

MAKES 4 SERVINGS

In the early days of the Heartland, onions were a staple. Every root cellar was filled each summer with sufficient stores to last until the next harvest. Pork was also popular and easy to come by since pigs were easy and cheap to raise—demanding nothing more than a barnyard and a few table scraps. Here the two come together in a farm-style casserole that's sure to please a hungry family.

4 extra-large yellow onions (about 14 ounces each), peeled
1 ⅓ cups water
⅔ cup long-grain white rice
1 pound ground pork
2 slices bacon, cut into ½-inch pieces
2 large garlic cloves, minced
2 large plum tomatoes, finely chopped (1 cup)

2 tablespoons tomato paste
2 tablespoons chopped fresh flat-leaf parsley
1 tablespoon chopped fresh thyme or 1 teaspoon dried, crumbled
Salt, optional, and freshly ground black pepper to taste
1 cup shredded Monterey Jack cheese (¼ pound)
1 cup half-and-half

PREP TIME: 40 MIN
BAKE TIME: 1–1 1/4 HR

1. Preheat oven to 325°F. Lightly butter a shallow 3-quart casserole and set aside.

2. Cut a slice from the root end of each onion so they stand upright. Cut off the top quarter of onions. Cut a cone shape into each onion and using a spoon, scoop out centers, leaving a shell about ¼ inch thick.

3. Finely chop onion centers and set aside. Cook onion shells in boiling water just until tender but still holding their shape, about 3 minutes. Using a slotted spoon, remove onions and drain upside down on paper towels.

4. In a medium saucepan, bring water to a boil. Stir in rice. Reduce heat, cover, and simmer for 10 minutes, until rice is almost tender. Drain well. Spread rice evenly over bottom of prepared casserole.

5. Meanwhile, in a large nonstick skillet, cook pork and bacon over medium-high heat until pork is no longer pink, about 5 minutes, breaking up meat with a wooden spoon. Drain off all fat. Add reserved chopped onion and garlic to skillet and cook, stirring frequently, for 5 minutes. Stir in tomatoes, tomato paste, parsley, and thyme. Taste and season with salt, if desired, and pepper. Remove from heat.

6. Arrange onion shells over rice. Spoon pork mixture into each onion, mounding it slightly. Sprinkle cheese over onions and rice and pour on half-and-half.

7. Bake, uncovered, for 1 to 1 ¼ hours, until onions are tender and rice is crusty brown. Serve right away.

1 serving: 722 calories, 38 g protein, 35 g total fat (16.7 g saturated), 65 g carbohydrates, 368 mg sodium, 126 mg cholesterol, 8 g dietary fiber

MIDWESTERN SHEPHERD'S PIE

MAKES 4 SERVINGS

My father's ancestors came to this country from London well before the Revolutionary War, eventually settling in Illinois. In 1872, they moved to Oklahoma where my paternal grandfather bought his first farm. I found this recipe for shepherd's pie in my aunt's kitchen notebook, marked as being my grandmother's recipe. I adapted it to good effect, using pork. The pie could also be made with ground beef. My mother made shepherd's pie with the leftovers of Sunday's pot roast. Serve a green salad alongside, make a fresh pot of coffee, and enjoy.

1 pound russet potatoes, peeled and cut into 2-inch cubes (3 cups)

1 ¼ pounds ground pork

1 medium carrot, peeled and sliced (¾ cup)

1 medium celery rib with leaves, chopped (¾ cup)

4 green onions, white part only, thinly sliced (½ cup)

2 tablespoons unbleached all-purpose flour

¼ cup water

2 cups fresh or frozen corn kernels

½ teaspoon dried marjoram, crumbled
Salt, optional, and freshly ground black pepper to taste

1 tablespoon butter, melted

¼ to ⅓ cup buttermilk

PREP TIME: 40 MIN

BAKE TIME: 30 MIN + 3–4 MIN TO BROIL

1. In a large saucepan, cook potatoes in water to cover until tender, about 15 minutes. Drain and transfer to a large bowl. Cover and keep warm.

2. Meanwhile, in a large nonstick skillet, cook pork over medium-high heat, breaking up meat with a wooden spoon, for about 5 minutes, until no longer pink. Drain off all fat. Add carrot, celery, and green onions and cook, stirring frequently, for 5 minutes.

3. In a small bowl, whisk together flour and water. Add to skillet and cook, stirring constantly, until mixture has thickened, about 5 minutes. Stir in corn, marjoram, salt, if desired, and pepper. Transfer mixture to a shallow round 2-quart casserole, pressing down lightly with a spoon.

4. Preheat oven to 350°F. Using a potato masher or electric mixer, mash the potatoes until they are completely smooth, adding the butter and ¼ cup buttermilk as you are mashing. If the mixture is still too thick (the potatoes should have a very soft consistency), add buttermilk, 1 tablespoon at a time, mashing until desired consistency.

5. Spoon or pipe (using a pastry bag fitted with a large star or plain tip) potato mixture around the edge of the meat mixture.

6. Bake casserole, uncovered, for 30 minutes, until heated through. Remove from oven and heat broiler. Broil 3 inches from heat source for 3 to 4 minutes, until potatoes are golden brown. Serve right away.

1 serving: 516 calories, 32 g protein, 25 g total fat (9.9 g saturated), 42 g carbohydrates, 165 mg sodium, 103 mg cholesterol, 5 g dietary fiber

SAUSAGE AND RICE CASSEROLE

MAKES 6 SERVINGS

This is a great casserole to serve after a nippy day of boating on one of the many crystal-clear lakes in the Heartland, a day of raking leaves, or most any other outdoor activity. I frequently leave the casserole on auto-bake so it has already cooked for half the time before we return. There's still time to toss a salad and bake a pan of biscuits.

1 ½ pounds sweet Italian sausage, casings removed and meat coarsely chopped
1 medium yellow onion; chopped (1 cup)
1 medium red bell pepper, seeded and chopped (1 cup)
2 medium celery ribs, chopped (1 cup)
1 teaspoon dried Italian seasoning, crumbled

1 cup long-grain white rice
1 14 ½-ounce can artichoke hearts, drained
2 10 ¾-ounce cans condensed cream of chicken soup
2 cups water
1 cup shredded mozzarella cheese (¼ pound)

PREP TIME: 30 MIN
BAKE TIME: 1 HR
STAND TIME: 5 MIN

1. Preheat oven to 350°F. Lightly butter a deep 3-quart casserole and set aside.
2. In a large skillet, cook sausage over medium-high heat until browned, stirring frequently, about 10 minutes. Drain off all fat. Add onion, bell pepper, celery, and seasoning and cook, stirring frequently, for 5 minutes. Stir in rice. Remove from heat and set aside.
3. Cut artichoke hearts in half lengthwise and arrange in bottom of prepared casserole. Spoon sausage mixture over artichokes.
4. In a medium bowl, whisk together soup and water. Pour over the sausage mixture.
5. Bake casserole, covered, for 30 minutes. Uncover and sprinkle with cheese. Bake, uncovered, for 30 minutes more, until rice is tender and cheese is melted. Remove from oven and let stand for 5 minutes before serving.

1 serving: 484 calories, 23 g protein, 25 g total fat (9.1 g saturated), 42 g carbohydrates, 1,479 mg sodium, 63 mg cholesterol, 4 g dietary fiber

OVERNIGHT CHEESE AND SAUSAGE CASSEROLE

MAKES 8 SERVINGS

This is my family's favorite casserole for a holiday brunch or for when we're entertaining weekend guests and serving a hearty late breakfast. I usually serve this casserole buffet style, offering a side dish of chopped tomato, onion, and cilantro, dressed with a lemon-olive oil vinaigrette. When everyone's lingering over coffee, I bring out a basket of homemade cookies and a bowl of berries.

2 pounds hot or sweet Italian sausage, casings removed and meat coarsely chopped

1 large red bell pepper, seeded and chopped (1½ cups)

1 medium yellow onion, chopped (1 cup)

2 large garlic cloves, minced

2 4-ounce cans chopped green chiles, drained

1 1-pound loaf homemade-style white bread, sliced ½ inch thick

3 cups shredded sharp Cheddar cheese (¾ pound)

7 large eggs

5 cups whole milk

1 tablespoon dry mustard

½ teaspoon freshly ground black pepper

¼ teaspoon cayenne pepper

**PREP TIME:
35 MIN**

**CHILL TIME:
AT LEAST 12 HR**

BAKE TIME: 1 HR

**STAND TIME:
15 MIN**

1. Lightly butter a 13 x 9 x 2-inch baking dish and set aside. In a large skillet, cook sausage over medium-high heat until browned, stirring frequently, about 10 minutes. Drain off all fat. Add bell pepper, onion, and garlic and cook, stirring frequently, for 5 minutes more. Remove from heat and stir in green chiles. Set aside.

2. Cut bread into 1-inch pieces. Spread half of bread over bottom of prepared casserole. Spoon half of sausage mixture over bread and cover with half of cheese. Layer with remaining bread, sausage mixture, then cheese.

3. In a large bowl, whisk eggs until frothy. Whisk in milk, mustard, black pepper, and cayenne. Pour mixture over casserole. Tightly cover and chill for at least 12 hours or overnight.

4. Preheat oven to 350°F. Bake casserole, uncovered, until puffed, edges are golden brown, and a tester inserted near center comes out clean, about 1 hour. Let cool on a wire rack for 15 minutes before cutting into squares to serve.

1 serving: 697 calories, 39 g protein, 41 g total fat (19.2 g saturated), 42 g carbohydrates, 1,286 mg sodium, 299 mg cholesterol, 3 g dietary fiber

CRABMEAT SOUFFLÉ

MAKES 4 SERVINGS

This is a perfect dish to serve for a special late-evening supper with chilled champagne. Soufflés are not hard to make; remember, however, that they wait for no one—although they are not as fragile as most cooks claim. Just have everything ready and your guests seated at the table when it's time for the soufflé to come out of the oven. This soufflé can be made in individual dishes or in one large one. Accompany with a salad of baby greens and thin slices of grilled Brie spread on slices of peasant-style bread.

5 tablespoons butter	¼ teaspoon cayenne pepper
¼ pound shiitake mushrooms, cleaned, stems discarded, and caps finely chopped (2 cups)	Salt, optional, and freshly ground black pepper to taste
2 shallots, minced (¼ cup)	1 cup shredded Swiss cheese (¼ pound)
5 tablespoons unbleached all-purpose flour	5 large eggs, separated
¾ cup whole milk	¾ pound fresh or thawed frozen lump crabmeat
⅓ cup dry white wine, dry sherry, or additional milk	

PREP TIME: 25 MIN

BAKE TIME: 25–30 MIN (SMALL) OR 35–40 MIN (LARGE)

1. Preheat oven to 350°F (if using small dishes) or 375°F (if using a large dish). Generously butter four 1½-cup soufflé dishes or a 2-quart soufflé dish and set aside.
2. In a large saucepan, melt butter over medium heat. Add mushrooms and shallots and sauté until liquid has evaporated, about 5 minutes. Stir in flour and gradually blend in milk and wine. Season with cayenne, salt, if desired, and pepper. Cook, stirring constantly, until mixture just comes to a boil and thickens, about 3 minutes.
3. Reserve 2 tablespoons cheese and add remaining cheese to pan. Cook, stirring constantly, until cheese is melted.
4. Remove from heat and add egg yolks, one at a time, whisking well after each addition. Stir in crabmeat. Set aside.
5. In a medium bowl, using an electric mixer or a whisk, beat egg whites until stiff peaks form. Stir one-third of egg whites into crabmeat mixture to lighten it. Using a rubber spatula, gently and thoroughly fold in the remaining egg whites.
6. Spoon mixture into prepared soufflé dish(es). Sprinkle top(s) with reserved cheese.
7. Bake small soufflés for 25 to 30 minutes or large soufflé for 35 to 40 minutes, both uncovered, until puffy and golden brown and center feels firm when pressed gently. Serve right away.

1 serving: 514 calories, 36 g protein, 31 g total fat (16.9 g saturated), 18 g carbohydrates, 559 mg sodium, 420 mg cholesterol, 1 g dietary fiber

SALMON STEAK CASSEROLE

MAKES 4 SERVINGS

The Great Lakes of the Heartland are now the home of coho salmon, which was introduced to the icy waters by conservationists in the mid-1960s. Here salmon steaks bake atop a bed of noodles for an easy, elegant casserole.

4 fresh salmon steaks (about 8 ounces each), cut 1 ½ inches thick
⅓ cup fresh lemon juice (2 small lemons)
6 ounces thin egg noodles (3 ¾ cups)
¼ cup pine nuts
⅓ cup dry unseasoned bread crumbs
1 small yellow onion, chopped (½ cup)

2 large garlic cloves, minced
2 tablespoons finely chopped flat-leaf parsley
½ teaspoon fennel seeds, crushed
   Salt, optional, and freshly ground black pepper to taste
¼ cup mayonnaise
⅓ cup freshly grated Parmesan cheese

PREP TIME: 40 MIN
BAKE TIME: 15–20 MIN

1. Put salmon steaks in a nonreactive shallow dish. Pour lemon juice over salmon and turn to coat. Cover and refrigerate for 30 minutes.

2. Meanwhile, cook noodles according to package directions. Drain well. Set aside.

3. Preheat oven to 400°F. Lightly butter a shallow 2-quart casserole and set aside. In a small nonstick skillet, toast pine nuts over medium heat, stirring constantly, for 3 to 5 minutes, until fragrant and golden. Remove from heat.

4. In a medium bowl, mix pine nuts, bread crumbs, onion, garlic, parsley, fennel, salt, if desired, and pepper. Set aside.

5. Arrange noodles over bottom of prepared casserole. Place salmon steaks over noodles and discard lemon juice.

6. Spread each steak with 1 tablespoon mayonnaise. Evenly distribute bread crumb mixture over mayonnaise and sprinkle with Parmesan cheese.

7. Bake casserole, uncovered, for 15 to 20 minutes, until fish flakes easily when tested with a fork and topping is well browned. Serve right away.

1 serving: 575 calories, 41 g protein, 27 g total fat (6.2 g saturated), 40 g carbohydrates, 375 mg sodium, 116 mg cholesterol, 2 g dietary fiber

SALMON LASAGNA ROLL-UPS

MAKES 4 SERVINGS

A delicious new way to prepare lasagna using canned salmon and frozen chopped spinach. This casserole is special enough for guests but also so easy to make you can fix it for family meals as well. The recipe easily doubles or triples for large groups.

- 8 dried lasagna noodles
- 1 10-ounce package frozen chopped spinach, thawed and squeezed dry
- 2 6-ounce cans pink salmon, rinsed, drained and any bones and skin removed
- 2 tablespoons butter
- 1 large garlic clove, minced
- 5 tablespoons unbleached all-purpose flour
- 2 ½ cups evaporated milk
- ⅛ teaspoon ground nutmeg
- ⅛ teaspoon cayenne pepper
  Salt, optional, and freshly ground black pepper to taste
- 1 ½ cups part-skim ricotta cheese
- 1 large egg, lightly beaten
- 2 green onions, white part plus 1 inch green tops, thinly sliced (¼ cup)
- ¼ cup freshly grated Parmesan cheese (1 ounce)
- 1 cup shredded part-skim mozzarella cheese (¼ pound)

PREP TIME: 50 MIN

BAKE TIME: 30–40 MIN

1. Cook lasagna noodles according to package directions. Drain well and set aside.
2. Meanwhile, in a medium bowl, mix spinach and salmon with a fork. Set aside.
3. In a large saucepan, melt butter over medium heat. Add garlic and sauté for 1 minute. Stir in flour and cook over low heat, stirring constantly, for 2 to 3 minutes. Slowly whisk in milk. Cook over medium heat, whisking constantly, until mixture just comes to a boil and thickens, about 5 minutes. Remove from heat and whisk in nutmeg, cayenne, salt, if desired, and pepper. Set aside.
4. In a small bowl, mix ricotta, egg, and green onions. Stir 1 cup sauce into the salmon mixture. Set aside.
5. Preheat oven to 350°F. On a sheet of waxed paper, put 2 cooked lasagna noodles side by side, slightly overlapping. Spread noodles with one-fourth ricotta mixture, then one-fourth salmon mixture. Sprinkle with 1 tablespoon Parmesan and 1 tablespoon mozzarella. Beginning with a narrow end, roll both noodles together, jelly-roll style, and place seam side down in a 13 x 9-inch baking dish. Prepare remaining 3 roll-ups in same manner. Spoon remaining sauce over all.
6. Bake, uncovered, for 20 to 25 minutes. Sprinkle evenly with remaining ¾ cup mozzarella and continue to bake another 10 to 15 minutes, until cheese melts and top is lightly browned. Serve right away.

1 serving: 829 calories, 56 g protein, 39 g total fat (21.6 g saturated), 64 g carbohydrates, 950 mg sodium, 191 mg cholesterol, 4 g dietary fiber

WHITEFISH CASSEROLE

MAKES 4 SERVINGS

Whitefish is a firm-textured, mild-flavored freshwater fish found primarily in icy streams that feed into the cold waters of the Great Lakes. Although there are still a few commercial fisheries processing whitefish in northern Wisconsin, most of the whitefish that we get comes from Canada. Sold fresh or frozen, whitefish is a member of the salmon family. If it's not available in your area, you can make the casserole with fillet of sole or orange roughy.

6 ounces small shell macaroni
1 medium celery rib, finely chopped
  (½ cup)
2 tablespoons coarsely grated white onion
½ cup water
½ cup dry white wine
1 pound whitefish fillets, cut 1 inch thick

1 8-ounce package cream cheese, softened
½ cup sour cream
2 hard-cooked large eggs, peeled and chopped
  Salt, optional, and freshly ground black
  pepper to taste
½ cup dry unseasoned bread crumbs
2 tablespoons butter, melted

**PREP TIME:
40 MIN**

**BAKE TIME:
20 MIN**

1. Lightly butter a deep 2-quart casserole and set aside.
2. Cook macaroni according to package directions. Drain well. Arrange half of macaroni over bottom of prepared casserole and sprinkle with celery and onion.
3. In a large skillet, combine water and wine. Add fish fillets and bring to a simmer over medium-high heat. Simmer, uncovered, for 10 minutes, until fish flakes easily when tested with a fork. Drain well, reserving poaching liquid. Coarsely flake fish.
4. Preheat oven to 350°F. In a medium bowl, whisk together cream cheese, sour cream, and poaching liquid. Stir in chopped egg, salt, if desired, and pepper. Spoon half of mixture over macaroni, then cover with flaked fish. Top with remaining macaroni and remaining cream cheese mixture.
5. In a small bowl, mix bread crumbs and melted butter. Sprinkle evenly over casserole.
6. Bake, uncovered, for 20 minutes, until top is lightly browned and mixture is bubbly. Serve right away.

1 serving: 735 calories, 38 g protein, 42 g total fat (21.9 g saturated), 45 g carbohydrates, 457 mg sodium, 267 mg cholesterol, 2 g dietary fiber

FISHERMAN'S PIE

MAKES 4 SERVINGS

Walleye is a favorite fish among anglers in the northern Heartland. A member of the perch family, it has snowy white meat that is mild-flavored, sweet, and tender. If your market doesn't have walleye (mine sells it only frozen), substitute another mild, firm-fleshed fish such as fillet of sole, whitefish, or red snapper. For a photo of this dish, see title page.

1 ½ pound sheet frozen puff pastry dough, thawed
1 large egg beaten with 1 tablespoon water
½ pound small new potatoes, scrubbed
¼ pound frozen pearl onions, about 1 cup
2 medium carrots, peeled and thinly sliced (1 ½ cups)
2 tablespoons butter
¼ pound fresh mushrooms, cleaned, trimmed, and sliced (1 ½ cups)

1 large garlic clove, minced
1 medium fennel bulb, trimmed, cored, and thinly sliced (2 cups)
2 plum tomatoes, chopped (⅔ cup)
1 8-ounce can tomato sauce
2 tablespoons fresh lemon juice
1 teaspoon capers, drained
1 ½ pounds fresh or thawed frozen walleye fillets, cut into 2-inch pieces

PREP TIME: 50 MIN
BAKE TIME: 25–30 MIN
STAND TIME: 10 MIN

1. Place puff pastry on a lightly floured work surface. Using a deep 3-quart casserole as a guide, trim dough to shape of casserole but 1 inch larger. Lightly butter casserole and set aside.
2. Using a sharp knife or small hors d'oeuvre cutter, cut out a small fish shape from center of pastry to allow steam to escape. Brush pastry with beaten egg. Transfer to a baking sheet and refrigerate.
3. Preheat oven to 375°F. Cook potatoes in boiling water to cover for 5 minutes, just until tender. Drain well and set aside. Cook onions and carrots in boiling water to cover for 5 minutes. Drain well and set aside.
4. In a large skillet, melt butter over medium heat. Add mushrooms and garlic and sauté until mushrooms are soft, about 5 minutes. Add fennel and sauté until all liquid is absorbed, about 5 minutes. Stir in tomatoes, tomato sauce, lemon juice, capers, and reserved potatoes, onions, and carrots.
5. Spoon half of vegetable mixture into prepared casserole. Arrange fish pieces over vegetables and cover with remaining vegetable mixture.
6. Remove pastry from refrigerator and place over filling. Turn edges under and crimp.
7. Bake casserole, uncovered, for 25 to 30 minutes, until filling is bubbly and crust is golden brown. Remove from oven and let stand on a rack for 10 minutes before serving.

Advance Preparation: Casserole may be made ahead through step 6, covered tightly, and refrigerated overnight or up to 24 hours. Bring to room temperature before baking.

1 serving: 386 calories, 32 g protein, 13 g total fat (4.9 g saturated), 35 g carbohydrates, 655 mg sodium, 173 mg cholesterol, 6 g dietary fiber

MISSISSIPPI RIVER BAKE

MAKES 6 SERVINGS

I was driving by myself through the Heartland one summer, and as I crossed the Mississippi River at St. Louis, I could see the Delta Queen, a majestic passenger riverboat, steaming upriver. With this book in mind, I began recording on my ever-present tape recorder my thoughts for a fish casserole that might be served onboard. Since the riverboat comes north from Natchez, I decided my fantasy dish would contain both shrimp and crab and lots of hot, spicy flavors.

2 tablespoons butter
1 large yellow onion, chopped (1 ½ cups)
3 large garlic cloves, minced
1 large green bell pepper, seeded and chopped (1 ½ cups)
1 medium celery rib with leaves, chopped (¾ cup)
1 tablespoon olive oil
2 tablespoons unbleached all-purpose flour
1 ½ cups dry white wine
4 medium tomatoes, chopped (4 cups)
2 tablespoons tomato paste
1 tablespoon hot paprika
1 tablespoon chopped fresh oregano leaves or 1 teaspoon dried, crumbled

1 ½ teaspoons fresh thyme leaves or ½ teaspoon dried, crumbled
Salt, optional, and freshly ground black pepper to taste
¾ teaspoon hot pepper sauce or to taste, plus additional for serving
1 pound medium shrimp, peeled and deveined
¾ pound lump crabmeat, picked over
2 cups water
1 cup long-grain white rice
1 tablespoon minced fresh flat-leaf parsley
1 tablespoon fresh lemon juice
Fresh thyme leaves for garnish, optional

PREP TIME: 55 MIN
BAKE TIME: 20 MIN

1. Preheat oven to 350°F. Lightly butter a shallow 3-quart casserole and set aside. In a large skillet, melt butter over medium heat. Add onion and garlic and sauté until onion is soft, about 5 minutes. Add bell pepper and celery and sauté for 5 minutes more. Using a slotted spoon, remove vegetables to prepared casserole.
2. Add oil to skillet and sprinkle with flour. Cook over medium heat, stirring constantly, for 3 minutes. Whisk in wine and cook, stirring constantly, for 5 minutes. Stir in tomatoes, tomato paste, paprika, oregano, thyme, salt, if desired, pepper, and hot pepper sauce. Remove from heat and set aside.
3. Arrange uncooked shrimp and crabmeat over vegetables in casserole. Cover with tomato mixture.
4. Bake casserole, uncovered, stirring often, until shrimp are pink and firm, about 20 minutes.
5. Meanwhile, in a medium saucepan, bring water to a boil. Add rice. Reduce heat, cover, and simmer for 15 minutes or until rice is tender and liquid is absorbed. Fluff rice with a fork.
6. Remove casserole from oven and stir in parsley and lemon juice. Serve right away over rice. Garnish each serving with fresh thyme, if desired, and pass additional hot pepper sauce to sprinkle over each serving.

1 serving: 397 calories, 29 g protein, 9 g total fat (3.2 g saturated), 40 g carbohydrates, 366 mg sodium, 168 mg cholesterol, 3 g dietary fiber

MICROWAVE SOLE CASSEROLE WITH GREEN TARTAR SAUCE

MAKES 4 SERVINGS

You'll love the ease of preparation of this casserole. Keep it in mind when you arrive home late from work or shopping and the family meal must be made quickly. Most every supermarket or fish market sells fillet of sole, but you can also use flounder or orange roughy.

2 medium carrots, peeled and thinly
   sliced (1 ½ cups)
1 large celery rib with leaves, thinly sliced
   (1 ⅓ cups)
1 small red bell pepper, seeded and thinly
   sliced (¾ cup)
2 plum tomatoes, chopped (⅔ cup)
4 shallots, thinly sliced (½ cup)
1 large garlic clove, minced
¼ cup minced fresh flat-leaf parsley
1 pound fillets of sole
½ cup dry white wine or grapefruit juice

Salt, optional, and freshly ground
   black pepper to taste
4 sprigs fresh tarragon for garnish, optional

GREEN TARTAR SAUCE

1 teaspoon white wine vinegar
¼ teaspoon dried tarragon, crumbled
½ cup mayonnaise
2 anchovy fillets, drained and coarsely chopped
2 tablespoons chopped fresh flat-leaf parsley
1 green onion, white part plus 1 inch
   green tops, sliced (2 tablespoons)
¼ teaspoon dry mustard
¼ teaspoon Worcestershire sauce

PREP TIME: 25 MIN

MICRO-COOK TIME: 10–12 MIN

1. Generously butter a 10-inch shallow microwave-safe casserole. In a medium bowl, mix carrots, celery, bell pepper, tomatoes, shallots, garlic, and parsley. Spread over bottom of casserole, cover with a sheet of waxed paper, and cook on HIGH (100% power) for 4 minutes. Stir vegetables.

2. Fold fish fillets in half crosswise and place over vegetables with thickest portions toward outer edges. Pour wine into casserole.

3. Cover with a sheet of waxed paper and cook on HIGH for 6 to 8 minutes, rotating dish halfway once, until fish flakes easily when tested with a fork. Season with salt, if desired, and pepper.

4. Meanwhile, make tartar sauce. In a food processor or blender, combine vinegar and tarragon and let stand for 2 minutes. Add mayonnaise, anchovies, parsley, green onion, mustard, and Worcestershire sauce. Process until smooth, about 1 minute. Spoon sauce into a serving bowl.

5. Garnish each fish fillet with a tarragon sprig, if desired. Serve casserole, passing sauce separately to spoon over each portion.

1 serving: 379 calories, 24 g protein, 24 g total fat (3.7 g saturated), 13 g carbohydrates, 388 mg sodium, 72 mg cholesterol, 3 g dietary fiber

MEATLESS SPECIALTIES

WITHOUT QUESTION, HEARTLANDERS are eating less meat than they did ten years ago, as they search for foods lower in fat and higher in fiber.

This chapter will give you an opportunity to create meatless casserole entrees for brunch, lunch, supper, or entertaining. Here you'll find manicotti stuffed with cheese and fresh spinach in a lively meatless tomato sauce redolent of fresh herbs, a savory combination of brown rice and Swiss chard baked in an egg-cheese custard, and an oven-hash made from garden fresh vegetables topped with plump cornmeal dumplings. If you entertain, the Blue Cheese Pie with Wild Rice Crust, Baked Chiles and Cheese, or the Barley-Stuffed Bell Peppers are sure to be favorites. All of these protein-rich casseroles are so tasty and satisfying that no one will miss the meat.

Remember, too, as with other casseroles, you can make many of these meatless recipes today and bake them tomorrow. Some may be eaten cold or at room temperature, and most are excellent when reheated and served again. Fresh bread and an interesting salad are the only accompaniments needed.

BARLEY-STUFFED BELL PEPPERS

MAKES 4 SERVINGS

I grow barley on my farm in western Kansas. A grain from the grass family, barley dates back to the Stone Age. Whole hulled barley can be found at natural foods stores, but it needs to be soaked before cooking. Here I use pearl barley, a form that cooks in just 15 minutes and is available in most supermarkets. Serve these colorful stuffed peppers for Sunday supper with an assortment of baby greens, thin slices of pear, and a generous sprinkling of toasted sunflower seeds.

1 ½ cups low-sodium chicken broth
½ cup pearl barley
3 tablespoons olive oil
1 small red onion, chopped (½ cup)
2 large garlic cloves, minced
3 plum tomatoes, diced (1 cup)
1 medium carrot, peeled and diced (¾ cup)
¼ cup minced fresh basil leaves
  or 4 teaspoons dried, crumbled

2 tablespoons minced fresh flat-leaf parsley
¼ cup golden raisins
  Salt, optional, and freshly ground
  black pepper to taste
4 large red bell peppers
⅓ cup dry unseasoned bread crumbs
⅓ cup freshly grated Parmesan cheese

**PREP TIME:
40 MIN

BAKE TIME:
50 MIN**

1. In a medium saucepan, bring broth to a boil. Stir in barley. Reduce heat, cover, and simmer, for 13 to 15 minutes, until barley is almost tender. Drain if necessary.

2. Meanwhile, in a large skillet, heat 1 tablespoon oil over medium heat. Add onion and garlic and sauté until onion is soft, about 5 minutes. Stir in cooked barley, tomatoes, carrot, basil, parsley, and raisins. Remove from heat. Taste and add salt, if desired, and pepper.

3. Preheat oven to 350°F. Lightly butter a baking dish just large enough to hold bell peppers snugly. Cut off a section from one side of each bell pepper and scrape out ribs and seeds. Spoon barley mixture into bell peppers, dividing it evenly and mounding the tops.

4. Arrange peppers in prepared dish. Sprinkle each with bread crumbs and cheese, then drizzle with the remaining 2 tablespoons oil. Cover with aluminum foil.

5. Bake, covered, for 35 minutes. Uncover and bake for 15 minutes more, until peppers are tender and lightly browned. Serve right away.

Advance Preparation: Casserole may be made ahead through step 4, covered tightly, and refrigerated overnight or up to 24 hours. Bring to room temperature before baking.

1 serving: 363 calories, 11 g protein, 14 g total fat (3.4 g saturated), 52 g carbohydrates, 268 mg sodium, 7 mg cholesterol, 9 g dietary fiber

BROWN RICE AND CHARD CASSEROLE

MAKES 6 SERVINGS

My mother grew chard in her garden. An old-fashioned vegetable, chard is a variety of sugar beets grown for its greens and not its roots. Swiss chard has crinkly green leaves and celerylike stalks. Rhubarb chard is slightly tangier in flavor and adds a touch of color to any dish with its red stalks and dark green leaves. Either variety could be used for this casserole. Substantial enough to serve with a refreshing fruit salad for a light supper, it would also be exquisite alongside grilled salmon or panfried whitefish when served in smaller portions.

2 cups long-grain brown rice
5 cups low-sodium chicken broth
2 tablespoons butter
1 medium yellow onion, quartered and thinly sliced (1 ½ cups)
1 jalapeño chile pepper, seeded and minced (2 tablespoons)
2 large garlic cloves, minced

2 pounds fresh Swiss chard, coarse stems discarded, leaves rinsed and coarsely chopped
4 large eggs, lightly beaten
1 cup evaporated milk
⅛ teaspoon cayenne pepper
Salt, optional, and freshly ground black pepper to taste
1 ½ cups shredded sharp Cheddar cheese (6 ounces)

PREP TIME: 45 MIN
BAKE TIME: 30–35 MIN

1. In a medium saucepan, bring rice and broth to a boil. Reduce heat, cover, and simmer until rice is tender and liquid is absorbed, about 30 minutes. Remove from heat and fluff rice with a fork. Set aside.

2. Meanwhile, preheat oven to 350°F. Lightly butter a shallow 3-quart casserole and set aside. In a large skillet, melt butter over medium heat. Add onion, jalapeño, and garlic and sauté until onion is soft, about 5 minutes. Add Swiss chard and cook, stirring frequently, for 2 minutes. Remove from heat and stir in cooked rice, eggs, milk, cayenne, salt, if desired, and pepper. Spoon rice mixture into prepared casserole. Top with Cheddar cheese.

3. Bake casserole, uncovered, for 30 to 35 minutes, until cheese melts and mixture is bubbly. Serve right away.

1 serving: 539 calories, 23 g protein, 23 g total fat (12.0 g saturated), 62 g carbohydrates, 667 mg sodium, 195 mg cholesterol, 5 g dietary fiber

NORTHERN FRONTIER CASSEROLE

MAKES 6 SERVINGS

Buckwheat was a field crop of the early settlers of the Heartland, particularly suited to the scarcely tilled soil and short growing season of the northern frontier farms. Although not really a grain, it does have a seed that can be ground into a very flavorful flour. Buckwheat hotcakes were filling fare for farmers, miners, and railroaders. When raw buckwheat is roasted, it's called kasha, the form used in this savory casserole. In this recipe kasha is combined with bulgur, wheat that has been steamed, dried, and cracked. The casserole can be served as the main dish for a meatless meal or, in smaller portions, with roasted fish or poultry. I can buy kasha and bulgur at my supermarket, but if you live in a more rural area, you may need to locate a natural food store.

2 tablespoons mild vegetable oil, such as canola
¼ pound fresh mushrooms, cleaned, trimmed, and chopped (1 ½ cups)
1 small yellow onion, chopped (½ cup)
1 large garlic clove, minced
2 cups kasha

1 ½ cups bulgur
5 cups boiling vegetable broth or water
Salt, optional, and freshly ground black pepper to taste
1 8-ounce package cream cheese, cubed, at room temperature

PREP TIME: 20 MIN
BAKE TIME: 1 1/4 HR

1. Preheat oven to 350°F. Lightly butter a deep 2 ½-quart casserole and set aside.
2. In a large skillet, heat oil over medium heat. Add mushrooms, onion, and garlic and sauté until vegetables are soft, about 5 minutes. Add kasha and bulgur and stir until well coated with oil, about 2 minutes.
3. Transfer mixture to prepared casserole. Add boiling broth. Season with salt, if desired, and pepper.
4. Bake casserole, covered, for 1 hour. Uncover and stir in cream cheese. Bake, uncovered, for 10 minutes more. Serve right away.

1 serving: 539 calories, 16 g protein, 21 g total fat (8.8 g saturated), 78 g carbohydrates, 344 mg sodium, 42 mg cholesterol, 10 g dietary fiber

SUMMER SQUASH PIE

MAKES 6 SERVINGS

Years ago Marshall Field's department store, a landmark of Chicago's Loop for more than a century, served a similar squash pie for lunch. The pastry is easy to make, especially in a food processor, and rather than being rolled, it is patted into place. Serve this with a salad for a light supper or cut into thin slivers to serve as party hors d'oeuvres.

PASTRY CRUST
- 1 cup unbleached all-purpose flour
- ¼ teaspoon salt
- 6 tablespoons (¾ stick) cold butter, cut into small pieces
- 3 tablespoons ice water
- 1 large egg yolk

FILLING
- 4 large eggs
- ½ cup sour cream
- 2 cups shredded sharp Cheddar cheese (¾ pound)
- 6 green onions, white part and 1 inch green tops, thinly sliced (¾ cup)
- ¼ teaspoon hot pepper sauce
  Salt, optional, and freshly ground black pepper to taste
- 1 medium zucchini, trimmed and thinly sliced (1 ½ cups)
- 1 medium yellow summer squash, trimmed and thinly sliced (1 ½ cups)
- 1 3-ounce can French-fried onions

PREP TIME:
35 MIN + 25 MIN
TO PREBAKE
PIE SHELL
BAKE TIME:
25–30 MIN
STAND TIME:
5 MIN

1. **To make pastry by hand:** In a medium bowl, mix flour and salt. Using a pastry blender or two knives, cut in butter until mixture resembles coarse crumbs. In a small bowl, whisk together water and egg yolk. Add to flour mixture and stir with a fork until flour clumps together to form a dough.
   To make pastry in a food processor: Place flour and salt in food processor and process for 1 second. Add butter and pulse on/off until mixture resembles coarse crumbs. In a small bowl, whisk together water and egg yolk. With motor running, add egg mixture through feed tube and process just until dough leaves side of bowl and forms a ball.
2. Gather dough into a ball and flatten into a disk. Wrap in plastic and chill for 10 minutes.
3. Preheat oven to 350°F. Pat dough into bottom and up sides of a 10-inch deep-dish pie pan or quiche pan. Crimp pastry edges. Line pastry shell with aluminum foil and fill with pie weights or dried beans. Bake for 15 minutes. Remove foil and weights. Bake 10 minutes more. Remove from oven and let cool on a wire rack.
4. **To make filling:** In a large bowl, whisk eggs until frothy. Whisk in sour cream. Stir in cheese, green onions, hot pepper sauce, salt, if desired, and pepper. Set aside.
5. Arrange zucchini slices alternating with yellow squash slices overlapping in concentric circles over bottom of cooled pie shell. Pour egg mixture over squash. Top with onions.
6. Bake, uncovered, for 25 to 30 minutes, until mixture is set and top is browned. Let cool on a wire rack for 5 minutes before cutting into wedges.

1 serving: 536 calories, 18 g protein, 40 g total fat (21.0 g saturated), 27 g carbohydrates, 619 mg sodium, 256 mg cholesterol, 2 g dietary fiber

VEGETABLE OVEN-HASH WITH CORNMEAL DUMPLINGS

MAKES 6 SERVINGS

When the farmers' markets or the garden is brimming with summer's bounty, remember this recipe. It makes a delightful vegetarian main course or a hearty side dish when you're grilling fish or chicken.

2 tablespoons mild vegetable oil, such as canola
1 medium yellow onion, finely chopped (1 cup)
2 large garlic cloves, minced
1 large red bell pepper, seeded and chopped (1 ½ cups)
1 medium carrot, peeled and chopped (¾ cup)
1 medium celery rib with leaves, chopped (¾ cup)
2 medium zucchini, trimmed and sliced (3 cups)
1 medium yellow summer squash, trimmed and sliced (1 ½ cups)
1 tablespoon minced fresh oregano leaves or 1 teaspoon dried, crumbled
1 teaspoon chili powder
½ teaspoon ground cumin

⅛ teaspoon cayenne pepper
Salt, optional, and freshly ground black pepper to taste
1 15-ounce can kidney beans, drained and rinsed
1 14 ½-ounce can plum tomatoes, chopped, undrained
⅓ cup dry white wine

CORNMEAL DUMPLINGS
1 ½ cups stone-ground yellow cornmeal
½ cup unbleached all-purpose flour
2 tablespoons freshly grated Parmesan cheese
1 ½ teaspoons baking powder
1 ½ teaspoons sugar
¾ cup whole milk
1 large egg
3 tablespoons butter, melted
2 tablespoons snipped fresh chives

PREP TIME: 40 MIN
BAKE TIME: 35–40 MIN

1. Preheat oven to 400°F. In a large skillet, heat oil over medium heat. Add onion and garlic and sauté until onion is soft, about 5 minutes. Add bell pepper, carrot, and celery and sauté for 5 minutes more.

2. Add zucchini, yellow squash, oregano, spices, salt, if desired, and pepper and cook, stirring frequently, for 1 to 2 minutes, until squash begins to soften. Stir in beans, tomatoes, and wine. Transfer mixture to a shallow 3-quart casserole. Bake casserole, covered, for 20 minutes.

3. **Meanwhile, make dumplings:** In a medium bowl, mix cornmeal, flour, Parmesan cheese, baking powder, and sugar. In a small bowl, whisk together milk, egg, and butter. Make a well in center of dry ingredients. Pour in egg mixture and add chives. Stir just until blended. Let batter stand for 5 minutes, until thickened.

4. Remove casserole from oven and spoon small mounds of dumpling batter around outer edge of casserole. Bake, uncovered, for 15 to 20 minutes, until dumplings are firm and dry and vegetables are tender. Serve right away.

1 serving: 429 calories, 14 g protein, 14 g total fat (5.4 g saturated), 62 g carbohydrates, 384 mg sodium, 57 mg cholesterol, 11 g dietary fiber

BLUE CHEESE PIE WITH WILD RICE CRUST

MAKES 8 SERVINGS

Maytag blue cheese is made in Newton, Iowa, by a member of the Maytag family, famous for manufacturing washing machines. It's available in some specialty cheese shops and by mail order (see Sources, page 142). Here the wonderful cheese flavors a rich pie that's baked in a crispy crust formed by wild rice. You could always substitute Roquefort, Danish blue, or Stilton with good results. Serve it with a green salad for a special luncheon or slice the pie into thinner pieces for an elegant hors d'oeuvre. The crust can be made the day before and refrigerated overnight.

WILD RICE CRUST

- 1¾ wild rice
- 5 cups water
- 2 large eggs
- ⅔ cup freshly grated Parmesan cheese (about 2½ ounces)
- 3 tablespoons fresh lemon juice (1 large lemon)
- ¼ cup (½ stick) butter, melted
- Salt, optional, and freshly ground black pepper to taste

CHEESE FILLING

- 1 tablespoon butter
- 1 medium yellow onion, thinly sliced and separated into rings (1½ cups)
- 1 medium leek, white part and 1 inch green tops, well rinsed and finely chopped (¾ cup)
- 4 large eggs
- 1½ cups half-and-half
- 1 tablespoon Dijon-style mustard
- 1 cup crumbled Maytag blue cheese (¼ pound)
- 1 tablespoon chopped fresh basil leaves or 1 teaspoon dried basil leaves, crumbled
- 1 tablespoon finely chopped fresh flat-leaf parsley
- Salt, optional, and freshly ground black pepper to taste

PREP TIME: 1 HR
BAKE TIME: 30 MIN
STAND TIME: 10 MIN

1. Preheat oven to 350°F. **To make crust:** In a medium saucepan, bring rice and water to a boil. Reduce heat, cover, and simmer for about 45 minutes, until rice is tender. Drain if necessary. In a large bowl, whisk 2 eggs until frothy. Whisk in Parmesan cheese, lemon juice, and melted butter. Stir in cooked rice. Taste and add salt, if desired, and pepper. Transfer mixture to a 10-inch pie pan. Press evenly into bottom and up sides of pan. Bake for 15 minutes, until crust starts to become crispy. Remove from oven and cool on a wire rack.

2. **Meanwhile, make filling:** In a large skillet, melt butter over medium heat. Add onion rings and leek and sauté until onion is soft, about 5 minutes. Remove from heat.

3. In a large bowl, whisk 4 eggs until frothy. Stir in onion mixture, half-and-half, mustard, blue cheese, basil, parsley, salt, if desired, and pepper until well blended.

4. Increase oven temperature to 375°F. Pour mixture into prebaked crust. Bake, uncovered, for 30 minutes, until filling is set. Remove from oven and let stand on a wire rack for 10 minutes before slicing into wedges.

1 serving: 407 calories, 18 g protein, 23 g total fat (13.2 g saturated), 33 g carbohydrates, 544 mg sodium, 213 mg cholesterol, 3 g dietary fiber

OVEN-BAKED SHIITAKE OMELET

MAKES 6 SERVINGS

My mother often made an omelet filled with vegetables, which she baked in the oven in a cast-iron skillet. Since she kept a large flock of chickens for an ever-ready supply of fresh eggs, her omelets were fantastic. The only part I didn't like about omelet night was being sent into the hen house to gather the eggs—the resident rooster and I shared a mutual dislike. I love shiitake mushrooms, which are available year-round in my supermarket. Once an import item from Asia, shiitakes are now cultivated in several Heartland states. Serve the omelet with a leafy green salad and seasonal fresh fruit for a simple but satisfying supper. If you happen to have any leftovers, take them to work the next day for an exquisite lunch.

¼ cup olive oil

2 medium russet potatoes, peeled and thinly sliced (2 cups)

1 medium yellow onion, thinly sliced (1 ½ cups)

1 large garlic clove, minced
Salt, optional, and freshly ground black pepper to taste

¼ pound fresh shiitake mushrooms, cleaned, stems discarded, and caps sliced (3 cups)

1 small eggplant (about ½ pound), unpeeled and thinly sliced

2 medium tomatoes, thinly sliced

1 tablespoon minced fresh basil leaves or 1 teaspoon dried, crumbled

1 tablespoon snipped fresh chives or green onion tops

1 ½ teaspoons minced fresh oregano leaves or ½ teaspoon dried, crumbled

1 teaspoon minced fresh thyme leaves or ¼ teaspoon dried, crumbled

1 cup shredded Swiss cheese (¼ pound)

12 large eggs

3 slices bacon, crisply cooked, drained, and crumbled, for garnish, optional
Chopped fresh parsley for garnish, optional

PREP TIME: 25 MIN

BAKE TIME: 45 MIN

1. Preheat oven to 450°F. Spread 2 tablespoons oil over bottom of a deep 12-inch cast-iron or other ovenproof skillet. Arrange potato and onion slices in skillet and sprinkle with garlic, salt, if desired, and pepper. Bake, uncovered, for 15 minutes.

2. Top potato and onions with mushrooms and eggplant. Drizzle with remaining 2 tablespoons oil. Bake for 10 minutes more. Remove from oven and cover with tomatoes, herbs, and cheese.

3. In a large bowl, whisk eggs until frothy. Season with salt, if desired, and pepper. Pour eggs over vegetables in skillet. Using a knife, slightly move layered vegetables to allow egg mixture to flow to bottom of casserole. Bake, uncovered, for about 20 minutes, until puffed, golden brown, and a knife inserted into center comes out clean. (Do not overcook; omelet should be firm but not dry.)

4. Garnish with crumbled bacon and chopped parsley. Cut into squares and serve hot or at room temperature.

1 serving: 399 calories, 21 g protein, 26 g total fat (8.1 g saturated), 21 g carbohydrates, 233 mg sodium, 444 mg cholesterol, 3 g dietary fiber

BAKED CHILES AND CHEESE

MAKES 6 SERVINGS

When I was driving through the Heartland one summer, I stopped at a restaurant just outside Columbus, Ohio, that offered Southwestern food. I ordered the baked cheese and chilies made from an intriguing blend of golden raisins, goat cheese, blue cheese, and Monterey Jack cheese. I failed to ask for the recipe, but this comes close. The chef had used poblano chilies, a narrow medium-hot dark pine-green chile that's about 4 to 5 inches in length. If your market doesn't carry fresh poblanos, substitute canned whole green chilies.

9 fresh poblano chile peppers
2 medium yellow onions, finely chopped
   (2 cups)
⅓ cup golden raisins
2 large garlic cloves, minced
1 cup shredded Monterey Jack cheese
   (¼ pound)
½ cup crumbled goat cheese (¼ pound)

½ cup crumbled blue cheese
   (2 ounces)
¼ cup fresh cilantro leaves, well packed
3 large eggs
¾ cup evaporated milk
3 tablespoons butter, melted
   Salt, optional, and freshly ground
   black pepper to taste

**PREP TIME:
55 MIN

BAKE TIME:
30 MIN**

1. Preheat broiler. Lightly butter a shallow 2-quart casserole and set aside.
2. Place chile peppers on a baking sheet. Broil until skins are charred and blistered, 10 to 15 minutes, turning chiles once. Transfer chiles to a plastic or brown paper bag, seal, and let stand for 10 to 15 minutes. Peel skins from chiles and cut in half lengthwise. Remove and discard stems and seeds. Set aside.
3. Meanwhile, in a medium bowl, mix onions, raisins, and garlic. Set aside. In another medium bowl, mix Monterey Jack, goat cheese, and blue cheese. Set aside.
4. Arrange 6 chile pepper halves in prepared casserole. Sprinkle with one-third of onion mixture and one-third of cheese mixture. Sprinkle with half of cilantro leaves. Repeat layers and sprinkle with remaining cilantro leaves. Top with remaining chiles, onion mixture, and cheese mixture.
5. In a medium bowl, whisk eggs until frothy. Whisk in evaporated milk, melted butter, salt, if desired, and pepper. Pour egg mixture evenly into casserole. Using a knife, slightly move layered chiles to allow egg mixture to flow to bottom of casserole.
6. Bake casserole, uncovered, for 30 minutes, until cheese is melted and bubbly and egg mixture is set when casserole is shaken gently. Serve right away.

1 serving: 414 calories, 21 g protein, 26 g total fat (15.9 g saturated), 27 g carbohydrates, 433 mg sodium, 175 mg cholesterol, 3 g dietary fiber

SIDE·DISH FAVORITES

VEGETABLES AND GRAINS ARE A fundamental part of Heartland cookery. From late spring until late fall, Heartland farmers literally take to the streets, turning empty lots, pedestrian malls, and town squares into open-air farmers' markets.

Throughout the Heartland, home gardeners are planting seeds brought to the region by pioneering relatives — seeds quite often secured through the Seed Saver's Exchange, a network of farmers and gardeners dedicated to the reintroduction and cultivation of heirloom vegetables (see Sources, page 142).

In this chapter vegetables play a starring role. Served as an accompaniment to meat, poultry, or fish, these side-dish casseroles reflect the way that Heartlanders cook vegetables and grains today.

Here you'll find a Spicy Eggplant Casserole that is nicely spiced and will complement most any grilled entree. The Barley and Wild Mushroom Casserole will become a regular addition to your meals and the Puffed Potato Bake is a dish that I'd happily eat any day. In all, there are fifteen dishes that will please vegetable and non-vegetable lovers alike.

BARLEY AND WILD MUSHROOM CASSEROLE

MAKES 4 SERVINGS

Since fresh morels are available for such a short period of time each spring (April to June), I rely on dried morels the remainder of the year. In this recipe the Heartland delicacy is combined with fresh shiitake mushrooms, golden raisins, and barley for a side dish to serve with roasted poultry or duck.

½ ounce dried morels
¼ pound fresh shiitake
   mushrooms, cleaned,
   stems discarded, and caps
   thinly sliced (3 cups)
 1 small yellow onion, finely
   chopped (½ cup)

¾ cup pearl barley
2 ¼ cups low-sodium chicken broth
⅓ cup golden raisins
 1 tablespoon butter, melted
 1 tablespoon minced fresh thyme
   leaves or 1 teaspoon dried,
   crumbled

**PREP TIME:
15 MIN + 30 MIN
TO SOAK
MUSHROOMS
BAKE TIME:
1 HR**

1. In a small bowl, soak morels in warm water to cover for 30 minutes. Drain well and chop.
2. Preheat oven to 400°F. Lightly butter a deep 2-quart casserole and set aside.
3. In a medium bowl, mix morels, shiitake mushrooms, onion, barley, broth, raisins, butter, and thyme. Transfer mixture to prepared casserole.
4. Bake casserole, covered, for 1 hour, until barley is tender and all liquid is absorbed. Fluff with a fork and serve right away.

1 serving: 253 calories, 7 g protein, 4 g total fat (2.2 g saturated), 50 g carbohydrates, 70 mg sodium, 8 mg cholesterol, 7 g dietary fiber

ROASTED ASPARAGUS CASSEROLE

MAKES 4 SERVINGS

Over the years I've had marginal success in growing asparagus in my home garden, but it grows wild alongside the creek on one of my Kansas farms. Whether gathered from the garden, the creek bed, or the market, asparagus is always a springtime joy. Roasting intensifies the flavor of any vegetable, and that's especially true of asparagus. Look for fat spears with very tight heads. Peeling the asparagus is optional, but it's prettier if you do. I think you'll like this dish. It's simple and doubles easily for a party.

1 ½ pounds fresh asparagus spears	2 tablespoons finely chopped red bell pepper
2 tablespoons olive oil	½ cup evaporated milk
2 shallots, finely chopped (¼ cup)	½ cup freshly grated Parmesan cheese (2 ounces)

PREP TIME:
30 MIN

BAKE TIME:
20 MIN

1. Preheat oven to 475°F. Snap off and discard woody ends of asparagus. If desired, peel each spear two-thirds of the way up with a vegetable peeler. Arrange asparagus in a single layer on a large baking pan. Brush asparagus with oil.

2. Roast for 5 to 8 minutes (depending on the thickness of stalks), until crisp-tender. Turn occasionally for even cooking and to avoid browning.

3. Lightly butter a shallow 3-quart casserole. Transfer asparagus to prepared casserole. Reduce oven temperature to 400°F.

4. Sprinkle asparagus evenly with shallots and bell pepper. Add evaporated milk and sprinkle with Parmesan cheese.

5. Bake casserole, uncovered, for 20 minutes, until asparagus is tender and cheese is lightly browned. Serve right away.

1 serving: 206 calories, 12 g protein, 13 g total fat (4.8 g saturated), 13 g carbohydrates, 271 mg sodium, 19 mg cholesterol, 4 g dietary fiber

BROCCOLI AND CAULIFLOWER CASSEROLE

MAKES 6 SERVINGS

Two of my favorite vegetables combine in this rich casserole, which makes a wonderful dish for a winter dinner when you're roasting meat or poultry.

1 ½ pounds broccoli, trimmed and broken into large florets

1 small head fresh cauliflower (about 1 pound), trimmed and broken into large florets

¼ cup (½ stick) butter

1 small yellow onion, finely chopped (½ cup)

3 tablespoons unbleached all-purpose flour

1 cup low-sodium chicken broth

1 cup whole milk or half-and-half

1 ½ cups shredded Swiss cheese (6 ounces)

⅛ teaspoon cayenne pepper
Salt, optional, and freshly ground black pepper to taste

4 slices bacon, crisply cooked, drained, and crumbled

½ cup finely chopped hazelnuts, optional

PREP TIME:
30 MIN
BAKE TIME:
20–30 MIN

1. Blanch broccoli in boiling water until bright green and crisp-tender, about 5 minutes. Drain well and set aside. Blanch cauliflower in boiling water until crisp-tender, about 5 minutes. Drain well and set aside.

2. Preheat oven to 350°F. In a large saucepan, melt butter over medium heat. Add onion and sauté until soft, about 5 minutes. Sprinkle with flour and stir until well blended. Slowly whisk in broth and milk. Cook over low heat, whisking constantly, until smooth and thickened, about 5 minutes. Stir in cheese until melted. Season with cayenne, salt, if desired, and pepper. Remove from heat.

3. Arrange broccoli and cauliflower in a shallow 3-quart casserole. Pour cheese sauce over vegetables.

4. Sprinkle casserole evenly with crumbled bacon and hazelnuts, if desired. Bake, uncovered, until top is lightly browned and mixture is bubbly, about 20 to 25 minutes. Serve right away.

1 serving: 293 calories, 16 g protein, 19 g total fat (11.3 g saturated), 17 g carbohydrates, 299 mg sodium, 55 mg cholesterol, 5 g dietary fiber

FRESH CORN PIE WITH CHEESE CHILI CRUST

MAKES 8 SERVINGS

Fresh cilantro gives this pie a terrific flavor. Cilantro, readily available in supermarkets throughout the Heartland and an herb that I grow in my garden, is a love-it-or-hate-it herb. If your family doesn't like its pungent flavor, substitute flat-leaf parsley. Serve this pie when you're grilling hamburgers or steaks and produce stands are full of freshly picked corn.

CHILI CHEESE CRUST
- 1 ½ cups unbleached all-purpose flour
- ½ teaspoon chili powder
- ⅛ teaspoon salt
- ¼ cup (½ stick) cold butter, cut into small pieces
- 2 tablespoons cold vegetable shortening
- ⅓ cup shredded sharp Cheddar cheese
- 3 to 4 tablespoons ice water

CORN FILLING
- 4 large eggs
- 1 cup half-and-half
- 2 cups fresh or thawed frozen corn kernels
- 1 2 ½-ounce can chopped green chilies, drained
- ¼ cup chopped fresh cilantro
- ¼ teaspoon ground cumin
- Salt, optional, and freshly ground black pepper to taste
- Paprika for garnish, optional

PREP TIME: 25 MIN + 1 1/4 HR TO CHILL AND PREBAKE CRUST

BAKE TIME: 50–60 MIN

STAND TIME: 5 MIN

1. **To make crust:** In a medium bowl, mix flour, chili powder, and salt. Using a pastry blender or two knives, cut in butter and shortening until mixture forms small clumps. Add cheese and work until mixture forms coarse crumbs. Sprinkle mixture with water, 1 tablespoon at a time, tossing with a fork until evenly moistened. Gather dough into a ball and flatten into a small disk. Wrap in plastic and chill for about 1 hour.

2. Preheat oven to 375°F. On a lightly floured surface, roll out dough to a fit a 10-inch quiche pan or deep-dish pie pan. Trim pastry and crimp edges. Prick bottom and sides of dough several times with a fork. Bake for 8 to 10 minutes, until pastry begins to brown. Let cool on a wire rack. Reduce oven temperature to 350°F.

3. **Meanwhile, make filling:** In a large bowl, whisk eggs until frothy. Whisk in half-and-half. Stir in corn, green chiles, cilantro, cumin, salt, if desired, and pepper. Pour mixture into cooled prebaked crust. Dust top lightly with paprika, if desired.

4. Bake, uncovered, for 50 to 60 minutes, until center is firm when shaken gently. Let stand for 5 minutes on a wire rack before cutting into wedges.

1 serving: 296 calories, 9 g protein, 17 g total fat (8.4 g saturated), 27 g carbohydrates, 199 mg sodium, 138 mg cholesterol, 2 g dietary fiber

MOTHER'S BAKED CORN

My mother used to make this savory corn pudding for almost every holiday. It's best made with corn cut fresh from the cob, but you can also use frozen or vacuum-packed canned corn kernels.

2 cups fresh or thawed frozen corn kernels
1 16-ounce can cream-style corn
1 2-ounce jar diced pimientos, drained
2 tablespoons coarsely grated white onion
1 tablespoon sugar
½ teaspoon salt

¼ teaspoon ground white pepper
1 tablespoon butter, melted
5 large eggs, separated
2 cups whole milk
28 saltine crackers, crushed (1 cup)

PREP TIME: 20 MIN

BAKE TIME: 50–60 MIN

1. Preheat oven to 375°F. Lightly butter a shallow 3-quart casserole and set aside.
2. In a large saucepan, blanch fresh corn in boiling water to cover for 5 minutes. (If using frozen corn, blanch for 1 minute.) Drain well and transfer to a medium bowl. Stir in cream-style corn, pimientos, onion, sugar, salt, if desired, white pepper, and butter. Add egg yolks and milk and mix well.
3. In a medium bowl, using an electric mixer or a whisk, beat egg whites until soft peaks form. (Do not overbeat.) Using a rubber spatula, stir one-third of the egg whites into the corn mixture, then gently fold in remaining egg whites and cracker crumbs.
4. Spoon mixture into prepared casserole and bake for 50 to 60 minutes, until center is set when dish is shaken gently. Serve right away.

1 serving: 297 calories, 12 g protein, 11 g total fat (4.6 g saturated), 40 g carbohydrates, 735 mg sodium, 193 mg cholesterol, 4 g dietary fiber

SPICY EGGPLANT CASSEROLE

My brother-in-law, Melvin Ryberg, grew up on a farm near Emporia, Kansas, and shares my fondness for spicy foods. Recently he's been experimenting with growing chile peppers in his small patio garden. This is his recipe for eggplant, nicely spiced with fresh chiles. Melvin likes to serve this casserole when he's barbecuing a turkey, but it's also terrific with almost any grilled meat or chicken.

2 small eggplants (about ¾ pound each)	2 tablespoons olive oil
Salt, optional, and freshly ground black pepper to taste	1 15-ounce can tomato sauce
1 medium yellow onion	1 2 ½-ounce can sliced black olives
1 Anaheim chile pepper, seeded	½ teaspoon ground cumin
1 jalapeño chile pepper, seeded	1 ½ cups shredded sharp Cheddar cheese (6 ounces)
1 large garlic clove	Sour cream for garnish, optional

PREP TIME: 1 HR
BAKE TIME: 25 MIN

1. Cut unpeeled eggplants into ½-inch-thick slices. Put slices on paper towels and sprinkle with salt, if desired, and pepper. Let stand for 30 minutes.

2. Preheat oven to 450°F. Meanwhile, finely chop onion, chile peppers, and garlic; set aside.

3. Arrange eggplant slices in a single layer on a large rimmed baking sheet. Brush with oil. Bake until eggplant is softened, about 20 minutes.

4. Meanwhile, in a medium saucepan, mix tomato sauce, onion, chile peppers, garlic, olives, and cumin. Bring to a boil over medium-high heat, stirring occasionally. Reduce heat and simmer, uncovered, for 10 minutes, stirring occasionally.

5. Reduce oven temperature to 350°F. Lightly butter a shallow 2-quart casserole. Arrange half of eggplant slices over bottom of prepared casserole. Top with half of sauce and half of cheese. Repeat layering remaining eggplant, sauce, and cheese.

6. Bake casserole, uncovered, for 25 minutes, until heated through and mixture is bubbly. Pass sour cream in a separate bowl to spoon onto each serving.

1 serving: 238 calories, 10 g protein, 15 g total fat (6.8 g saturated), 18 g carbohydrates, 693 mg sodium, 30 mg cholesterol, 5 g dietary fiber

SWEET AND SOUR GREEN BEAN CASSEROLE

MAKES 8 SERVINGS

These beans are cooked the old-fashioned way, slowly until melt-in-your-mouth tender. Cooked this way, they are no longer the bright emerald color of crisp-cooked beans, but the flavor is wonderful. Whenever I serve ham, I freeze the scraps to use in this dish. The sweet, salty ham along with the salty cashews adds a nice finish to the dish.

2 pounds fresh green beans, trimmed
1 tablespoon mild vegetable oil, such as canola
1 medium yellow onion, chopped (1 cup)
2 large garlic cloves, thinly sliced
1 medium red bell pepper, seeded and
    cut into thin julienne strips (1 ½ cups)
    Salt, optional, and freshly ground
    black pepper to taste

1 14 ½-ounce can stewed tomatoes
2 ounces ham, cut into thin strips (⅓ cup)
⅓ cup white wine vinegar
¼ cup packed light brown sugar
1 tablespoon Worcestershire sauce
½ teaspoon dry mustard
⅓ cup salted cashews

**PREP TIME:
35 MIN
BAKE TIME:
35–45 MIN**

1. Preheat oven to 350°F. Lightly butter a shallow 2-quart casserole and set aside.

2. Blanch beans in boiling water to cover until crisp-tender, about 5 minutes. Drain well and transfer to prepared casserole.

3. In a large skillet, heat oil over medium heat. Add onion and garlic and sauté until onion is soft, about 5 minutes. Add bell pepper and sauté until beginning to soften, about 2 minutes. Transfer mixture to casserole. Season with salt, if desired, and pepper.

4. Add tomatoes, ham, vinegar, brown sugar, Worcestershire sauce, and mustard to skillet and cook over medium heat, stirring frequently, for 5 minutes. Spoon mixture over beans.

5. Bake casserole, covered, for 35 to 45 minutes, until heated through and bubbly. Sprinkle with cashews and serve right away.

Advance Preparation: Casserole may be made ahead through step 4, covered tightly, and refrigerated overnight or up to 24 hours. Bring to room temperature before baking.

1 serving: 144 calories, 6 g protein, 5 g total fat (0.8 g saturated), 22 g carbohydrates, 292 mg sodium, 4 mg cholesterol, 6 g dietary fiber

BAKED SUGAR PUMPKIN WITH APPLES AND MAPLE SYRUP

MAKES 8 SERVINGS

Pumpkins were a popular vegetable in the early days of the Heartland, frequently boiled and mashed like potatoes, seasoned with salt, pepper, and butter. Pumpkins were also pressed for syrup, simmered for pumpkin butter, and roasted and ground for coffee. Pumpkins for eating, called sugar or cheese pumpkins, are small, with a deep, rich flavor and a meaty texture. Here I've baked a sugar pumpkin with sautéed apples and maple syrup for a casserole to serve with holiday ham or turkey or almost any roasted meat. You can also make this casserole using butternut, Hubbard, acorn, or turban winter squash in place of the sugar pumpkin.

1 sugar pumpkin (about 4 pounds)
6 tablespoons (¾ stick) butter at room temperature
4 medium Jonathan apples, peeled, cored, and sliced (4 cups)
3 tablespoons pure maple syrup

Salt, optional, and freshly ground black pepper to taste

PECAN TOPPING
2 cups cornflakes, coarsely crushed
⅓ cup chopped pecans
3 tablespoons butter, melted

**PREP TIME:
15 MIN + 50 MIN
TO BAKE PUMPKIN
BAKE TIME:
30–35 MIN**

1. Preheat oven to 350°F. Cut pumpkin in half lengthwise. Scrape out seeds and membrane. Place cut side down on a foil-lined baking sheet. Bake for 50 minutes, until tender.
2. Meanwhile, lightly butter a shallow 3-quart casserole. In a large skillet, melt 3 tablespoons butter over medium heat. Add apples and sauté until barely tender, about 5 minutes. Spoon apples into prepared casserole.
3. Remove baking sheet from oven and let pumpkin cool enough to remove charred skin. Cut pumpkin into 1-inch pieces. Arrange pumpkin over apples in casserole.
4. In same skillet, melt remaining 3 tablespoons butter over medium heat. Stir in maple syrup until thoroughly blended. Spoon mixture over pumpkin. Season with salt, if desired, and pepper.
5. **To make topping:** In a medium bowl, mix cornflakes, pecans, and butter. Sprinkle mixture evenly over casserole. Bake casserole, uncovered, at 350°F for 30 to 35 minutes, until heated through and top is lightly browned. Serve right away.

Advance Preparation: Casserole may be made ahead through step 4, covered tightly, and refrigerated overnight or up to 24 hours. Bring to room temperature before topping and baking.

1 serving: 247 calories, 2 g protein, 17 g total fat (8.4 g saturated), 25 g carbohydrates, 198 mg sodium, 35 mg cholesterol, 3 g dietary fiber

SWEET POTATO BAKE WITH MINCEMEAT

MAKES 8 SERVINGS

Each year in early November my mother made mincemeat, which she canned in mason jars. A means of preserving meat and game in earlier times, mincemeat in our house usually ended up in holiday pies, but occasionally Mother would make a casserole of sweet potatoes and mincemeat baked in orange juice. Her recipe was lost long ago, but after several tries I've come up with a version that's close. Although mincemeat is not hard to make, I don't bother since this recipe needs so little. Instead I buy small jars of the rich, spicy preserve from a specialty food store. I add a small amount of brandy to the casserole, but you could also use extra orange juice.

8 medium sweet potatoes, scrubbed	1 ½ cups fresh orange juice (about 5 oranges)
¾ cup mincemeat	⅓ cup brandy or additional orange juice
½ cup (¼ cup) butter	1 teaspoon grated orange rind
2 tablespoons unbleached all-purpose flour	½ cup pecan halves, optional

PREP TIME: 30 MIN
BAKE TIME: 30 MIN

1. Boil sweet potatoes in water to cover until tender, about 20 minutes. Drain well and let cool. When cool enough to handle, peel sweet potatoes and cut into ½-inch-thick slices.
2. Preheat oven to 325°F. Lightly butter a shallow 3-quart casserole. Spread mincemeat evenly over bottom of prepared casserole. Arrange sweet potato slices over mincemeat.
3. In a small saucepan, melt butter over medium heat. Stir in flour. Slowly whisk in orange juice and cook, whisking constantly, until smooth and slightly thickened, about 5 minutes. Whisk in brandy and orange rind. Pour mixture over sweet potatoes and sprinkle with pecans if desired.
4. Bake casserole, uncovered, for 30 minutes, until heated through and bubbly. Serve right away.

Advance Preparation: Casserole may be made ahead through step 3, covered tightly, and refrigerated overnight or up to 24 hours. Bring to room temperature before baking.

1 serving: 371 calories, 4 g protein, 11 g total fat (4.1 g saturated), 60 g carbohydrates, 158 mg sodium, 16 mg cholesterol, 4 g dietary fiber

SUMMER TOMATO PIE

MAKES 6 SERVINGS

The Pillsbury Company, headquartered in Minneapolis, Minnesota, hosted the first national baking competition in 1949. First named the Grand National Recipe and Baking Contest, the annual event quickly became known as (and still is) the Bake-Off. I never entered the contest (and couldn't once I started working as a food writer), but I've often thought that my recipe for tomato pie would be a winner. It has garnered lots of compliments over the years.

1 10-ounce can refrigerated buttermilk biscuits
2 pounds ripe tomatoes
1 teaspoon dried oregano leaves, crumbled
   Salt, optional, and freshly ground black pepper to taste

1 cup shredded sharp Cheddar cheese (¼ pound)
½ cup mayonnaise
1 small yellow onion, finely chopped (½ cup)
1 4-ounce can chopped green chiles, drained

PREP TIME:
20 MIN
BAKE TIME:
20–25 MIN

1. Preheat oven to 425°F. Lightly butter a 10-inch pie pan. Remove biscuit dough from can and press evenly over bottom and up sides of prepared pan, sealing splits between biscuits.
2. Peel and thinly slice tomatoes. Arrange tomato slices over dough, overlapping slightly. Sprinkle with oregano, salt, if desired, and pepper.
3. In a medium bowl, combine cheese, mayonnaise, onion, and chiles. Spread mixture over tomatoes to cover completely.
4. Bake pie, uncovered, for 20 to 25 minutes, until golden brown. Serve warm.

1 serving: 299 calories, 7 g protein, 21 g total fat (5.9 g saturated), 23 g carbohydrates, 608 mg sodium, 23 mg cholesterol, 2 g dietary fiber

COUNTRY TURNIP AND POTATO BAKE

MAKES 6 SERVINGS

Turnips were one of the early settlers' most important crops since they kept well in the root cellar and lasted long into the winter. In this casserole turnips bake with potatoes and garlic for a rustic dish to serve with roasted pork or lamb.

1 pound small white turnips, peeled and thinly sliced

3 large garlic cloves, thinly sliced

1 pound thin-skinned potatoes, peeled and thinly sliced

1 teaspoon minced fresh tarragon leaves or ¼ teaspoon dried, crumbled

½ teaspoon minced fresh thyme leaves or ⅛ teaspoon dried, crumbled

Salt, optional, and freshly ground black pepper to taste

1 cup half-and-half

1 tablespoon butter

PREP TIME: 35 MIN
BAKE TIME: 45–55 MIN
STAND TIME: 5 MIN

1. Preheat oven to 325°F. Butter a shallow 2-quart casserole.

2. Layer half of turnips, garlic, and potatoes over bottom of prepared casserole. Sprinkle with herbs, salt, if desired, and pepper. Repeat, using remaining turnips, garlic, and potatoes. Pour cream over vegetables and dot with butter.

3. Bake casserole, uncovered, for 45 to 55 minutes, until vegetables are tender and cream has been absorbed. Remove from oven and cool on a wire rack for 5 minutes before cutting into wedges.

1 serving: 142 calories, 3 g protein, 7 g total fat (4.1 g saturated), 18 g carbohydrates, 85 mg sodium, 20 mg cholesterol, 3 g dietary fiber

NORTH WOODS WILD RICE WITH CRANBERRIES AND PECANS

MAKES 8 SERVINGS

The nutty-flavored wild rice combines with mushrooms, dried cranberries, and toasted pecans for a spectacular rice pilaf to serve at your next holiday gathering or family celebration. Look for the dried cranberries in the produce section of your supermarket or specialty food store. Minnesota wild rice and dried cranberries are also available by mail order (see Sources page 142).

2 cups wild rice, rinsed
2 quarts low-sodium chicken broth
1 cup pecan halves
¼ cup (½ stick) butter
2 medium yellow onions, finely chopped (2 cups)
2 medium celery ribs with leaves, thinly sliced (1 ½ cups)
1 cup dried cranberries
1 tablespoon chopped fresh marjoram leaves or 1 teaspoon dried, crumbled

1 tablespoon chopped fresh sage leaves or 1 teaspoon dried, crumbled
1 tablespoon chopped fresh thyme leaves or 1 teaspoon dried, crumbled
3 tablespoons grated orange rind (1 medium orange)
Salt, optional, and freshly ground black pepper to taste
Julienne strips of orange peel for garnish, optional

**PREP TIME:
20 MIN + 45 MIN
TO COOK RICE
BAKE TIME:
30–35 MIN**

1. In a large saucepan, combine wild rice and broth. Bring to a boil over high heat. Reduce heat, cover, and simmer for about 45 minutes, until rice is almost tender. Drain if necessary.
2. Meanwhile, preheat oven to 350°F. Spread pecans in a single layer in a baking pan. Toast in oven for 7 to 10 minutes, stirring occasionally. Remove from oven, let cool slightly, and coarsely chop. Set aside.
3. In a large skillet, melt butter over medium heat. Add onions and celery and sauté until soft, about 5 minutes. Remove from heat and stir in cranberries, toasted pecans, herbs, and orange rind. Add wild rice and toss gently to combine. Taste and add salt, if desired, and pepper.
4. Reduce oven temperature to 325°F. Lightly butter a shallow 3-quart casserole. Transfer rice mixture to prepared casserole.
5. Bake casserole, covered, for 30 to 35 minutes, until heated through. Sprinkle with orange peel and serve right away.

Advance Preparation: Casserole may be made ahead through step 4, covered tightly, and refrigerated overnight or up to 24 hours. Bring to room temperature before baking.

1 serving: 392 calories, 11 g protein, 18 g total fat (5.4 g saturated), 50 g carbohydrates, 191 mg sodium, 19 mg cholesterol, 5 g dietary fiber

BAKED WINTER FRUIT CASSEROLE

MAKES 8 SERVINGS

Remember this spicy casserole the next time you're baking a ham or roasting a turkey or chicken—especially during the cold winter months when fresh fruit is scarce or expensive. It's equally terrific for breakfast or brunch.

1 large pink grapefruit
1 large navel orange
4 slices fresh or canned juice-packed pineapple slices
1 large Golden Delicious apple, unpeeled, cored, and cut into ½-inch-thick wedges
1 large ripe Bosc pear, unpeeled, cored, and cut into ½-inch-thick wedges
2 medium ripe bananas, peeled and thickly sliced

3 tablespoons butter at room temperature
½ cup packed light brown sugar
½ cup fresh orange juice (about 2 oranges)
2 tablespoons fresh lemon juice
½ teaspoon ground cinnamon
⅛ teaspoon ground cloves
⅛ teaspoon ground nutmeg

PREP TIME: 35 MIN
BAKE TIME: 30–35 MIN

1. Preheat oven to 375°F. Lightly butter a shallow 3-quart casserole and set aside.
2. Using a sharp knife, cut peel and white pith from grapefruit and orange. Holding each over a large bowl to catch juice, remove sections by sliding knife down one side of section toward center and cutting it away from membrane. Twist blade, lift out sections, and add to bowl.
3. Cut each pineapple slice into quarters and add to bowl. Add apple, pear, and bananas and toss gently to mix. Transfer fruits to prepared casserole.
4. In a small saucepan, combine butter, brown sugar, orange juice, lemon juice, and spices. Cook, stirring constantly, until sugar is dissolved, about 4 minutes. Pour mixture over fruit.
5. Bake casserole, covered, for 20 minutes. Uncover and bake until fruit is tender and mixture is bubbly, 10 to 15 minutes more. Serve right away.

1 serving: 166 calories, 1 g protein, 5 g total fat (2.8 g saturated), 32 g carbohydrates, 49 mg sodium, 12 mg cholesterol, 3 g dietary fiber

POTLUCK PLEASERS

POTLUCKS ARE AS POPULAR AS ever in the Heartland, where one is likely to be invited to one or more a month. Happily, casseroles are a natural solution for these gatherings since they are easy to transport and economical.

When taking a casserole to someone else's house, you might want to partially bake the casserole at home, then finish the baking at the site of the potluck dinner. Otherwise you'll need to keep the just-baked casserole hot by first wrapping the casserole immediately in foil, then placing it in a cloth-lined or newspaper-lined cardboard carton. In either case, transport the casserole on the floor or trunk of your car, making sure that it stays level and immobile.

In this chapter you'll find simple-to-make casseroles such as Linda's Chicken Spaghetti and Country Macaroni and Cheese. Others, such as the Duck Cassoulet or Pizza Potpie, require more preparation, but the raves they will receive more than make up for the extra effort. There are even two decadent casserole desserts. In all, there are ten portable casseroles to share with family and friends.

VEGETABLE LASAGNA WITH MEAT SAUCE

MAKES 12 SERVINGS

This rustic version of classic lasagna is made with dried lasagna noodles; but if you own a pasta machine, by all means use it to make fresh lasagna noodles.

VEGETABLE LAYER
2 large red bell peppers (about 1 pound)
1 medium eggplant (about 1 pound)

MEAT SAUCE
1 tablespoon mild vegetable oil,
  such as canola
2 medium yellow onions, finely chopped
  (2 cups)
2 large garlic cloves, minced
1 ½ pounds extra-lean ground beef
1 28-ounce can crushed tomatoes in puree
1 16-ounce can tomato sauce
1 6-ounce can tomato paste
1 cup water

¾ cup dry red wine or additional water
2 tablespoons chopped fresh basil leaves
  or 2 teaspoons dried, crumbled
1 tablespoon chopped fresh oregano leaves
  or 1 teaspoon dried, crumbled
  Salt, optional, and freshly ground
  black pepper to taste

THE OTHER LAYERS
1 ½ pounds dried lasagna noodles
3 cups part-skim ricotta cheese, drained
  (1 ½ pounds)
1 pound part-skim mozzarella cheese,
  thinly sliced
1 cup freshly grated Parmesan cheese (¼ pound)

**PREP TIME:
1 1/2 HR
BAKE TIME:
30-40 MIN
STAND TIME:
5-10 MIN**

1. Preheat boiler. Line a large baking sheet with foil. Place bell peppers on prepared baking sheet. Broil until skins are charred and blistered, 10 to 15 minutes, turning once. Transfer peppers to a plastic or brown paper bag, seal, and let stand for 10 to 15 minutes. Peel skins from peppers and cut in half lengthwise. Remove and discard stems and seeds. Cut peppers lengthwise into 1-inch wide strips. Set aside.

2. Meanwhile, trim unpeeled eggplant and cut lengthwise into ½-inch thick slices. Re-line baking sheet with foil. Place eggplant slices in a single layer on prepared baking sheet. Broil 3 to 4 inches from heat source until lightly browned, 6 to 8 minutes, turning once. Remove from oven and set aside.

3. **To make sauce:** In a large skillet, heat oil over medium heat. Add onions and garlic and sauté until onions are soft, about 5 minutes. Add beef and cook, breaking up meat with a wooden spoon, for about 10 minutes, until no longer pink. Discard all fat. Stir in crushed tomatoes, tomato sauce, tomato paste, water, wine, herbs, salt, if desired, and pepper until blended. Simmer, uncovered, until sauce begins to thicken, about 15 minutes.

4. Meanwhile, cook noodles according to package directions. Drain well, rinse in cold water, and drain again.

5. Spoon 1 cup of meat sauce evenly over bottom of a 16 x 12-inch casserole. Arrange one-third of noodles over sauce. Arrange half of eggplant slices and half of bell pepper strips over noodles. Gently spread one-third of remaining meat sauce over vegetables. Top with one-third of ricotta, then one-third of mozzarella. Repeat layers once. Top with remaining noodles, remaining sauce, and remaining ricotta and mozzarella. Sprinkle with Parmesan.

6. Preheat oven to 350°F. Bake, uncovered, for 30 to 40 minutes, until filling is bubbly and lasagna is heated through. Remove from oven and let stand for 5 to 10 minutes before cutting into squares.

Advance Preparation: Lasagna may be made ahead through step 5, covered tightly, and refrigerated overnight or up to 24 hours. Bring to room temperature before baking.

1 serving: 631 calories, 42 g protein, 23 g total fat (11.4 g saturated), 63 g carbohydrates, 1,003 mg sodium, 81 mg cholesterol, 5 g dietary fiber

LINDA'S CHICKEN SPAGHETTI

MAKES 12 SERVINGS

I must admit that I did not grow up on chicken spaghetti, but my friend Linda Fleming did. A native of Oklahoma, Linda claims that every time she visits Oklahoma City she makes and freezes a dozen or so casseroles of chicken spaghetti for her parents to eat until her next visit. Linda's version contains a goodly amount of fresh basil, an appropriate addition since she lectures on growing herbs at the New York Botanical Garden.

1 whole chicken (4 pounds),
   cut into 8 pieces, rinsed, and patted dry,
   giblets discarded
2 quarts water
1 ¼ pounds dried spaghetti
⅓ cup butter
1 large green bell pepper, seeded and
   finely chopped (1 ½ cups)
1 large yellow onion, chopped
   (1 ½ cups)
3 large celery ribs with leaves, chopped
   (4 cups)
3 large garlic cloves, minced

½ pound fresh mushrooms, cleaned,
   trimmed, and sliced (3 cups)
   Salt, optional, and freshly ground
   black pepper to taste
1 18-ounce can tomato paste
1 16-ounce can tomato sauce
1 tablespoon Worcestershire sauce
1 2 ½-ounce can sliced black olives, drained
¼ cup chopped fresh basil leaves
   or 4 teaspoons dried, crumbled
3 cups shredded sharp Cheddar cheese
   (¾ pound)
¼ cup freshly grated Parmesan cheese

**PREP TIME:
1 1/4 HR
BAKE TIME:
1 HR**

1. In a 4-quart pot, simmer chicken in water over medium heat until chicken is tender, about 35 minutes. Using a slotted spoon, transfer chicken pieces to a platter and let cool. Strain chicken stock and return to pot.
2. Bring stock to a boil. Add spaghetti and boil for 5 minutes. Drain well and set aside.
3. When chicken is cool enough to handle, discard skin and remove meat from bones. Chop meat into bite-size pieces. Set aside.
4. In a 6-quart Dutch oven, melt butter over medium heat. Add bell pepper, onion, celery, and garlic and sauté until vegetables are beginning to soften, about 5 minutes. Add mushrooms and sauté over medium-high heat for 5 minutes, until liquid is absorbed. Season with salt, if desired, and pepper. Stir in tomato paste, tomato sauce, Worcestershire sauce, and olives. Reduce heat and simmer, uncovered, for 10 minutes. Stir in cooked chicken and basil.
5. Preheat oven to 350°F. Lightly butter a deep 4-quart casserole. Layer half of spaghetti over bottom of casserole. Spoon half of chicken mixture over spaghetti and sprinkle evenly with half of cheese. Repeat layers once.
6. Bake casserole, uncovered, for 1 hour, until lightly browned filling is bubbly. Serve warm.

1 serving: 534 calories, 36 g protein, 21 g total fat (10.8 g saturated), 52 g carbohydrates, 971 mg sodium, 100 mg cholesterol, 5 g dietary fiber

DUCK CASSOULET

MAKES 16 SERVINGS

There are many versions of cassoulet. This one appears involved, but actually it goes together quite easily and calls for smoked duck, chicken, or turkey. If you don't have a hunter in the family (or a backyard smoker), you can buy both smoked duck and chicken at specialty food markets or by mail order (see Sources, page 142). Cassoulet is a particularly festive dish to serve during the holidays for a gathering of family and friends.

4 cups dried navy beans, picked over and well rinsed
4 quarts water
1 pound bacon, cut into 1-inch pieces
1 cup boiling water
2 medium yellow onions, chopped (2 cups)
2 medium carrots, peeled and chopped (1 ½ cups)
8 fresh flat-leaf parsley sprigs
6 large garlic cloves, peeled
2 large bay leaves
2 sprigs fresh thyme
4 whole cloves
½ teaspoon ground allspice
4 pounds boneless smoked duck, chicken or turkey, cut into 2-inch chunks

1 pound smoked Polish sausage, sliced ¼ inch thick
2 tart apples such as Granny Smith, Ida Red, or Prairie Spy, peeled, cored, and cut into ½-inch pieces (2 cups)
3 large plum tomatoes, chopped (1 ½ cups)
1 10 ¼-ounce can condensed chicken broth
1 6-ounce can tomato paste
1 cup dry red wine
¾ cup brandy
1 teaspoon freshly ground black pepper

BREAD CRUMB TOPPING
4 cups fresh bread crumbs
1 cup chopped fresh flat-leaf parsley
6 tablespoons (¾ stick) butter, melted

PREP TIME: 45 MIN + AT LEAST 1 1/2 HR TO SOAK BEANS

COOK AND BAKE TIME: 2 1/2 HR

1. In an 8-quart Dutch oven, cover beans with water. Soak overnight or for at least 6 hours. Or, bring to a boil over high heat and boil, uncovered, for 15 minutes. Remove from heat, cover, and let stand for 1 hour.

2. In a large skillet, blanch bacon in boiling water for 2 minutes. Drain off and discard liquid. Return bacon to skillet and add onions and carrots. Cook, stirring constantly, over medium heat until onion is soft, about 5 minutes. Using a slotted spoon, transfer bacon and vegetables to Dutch oven.

3. Tie the parsley sprigs, garlic, bay leaves, thyme, cloves, and allspice in a small square of cheesecloth. Add to Dutch oven.

4. Bring bean mixture to a boil over high heat. Reduce heat to medium, partially cover, and simmer for 1 hour. Drain bean mixture and discard herb bag.

5. Preheat oven to 325°F. Return bean mixture to Dutch oven. Add duck, sausage, apples, and tomatoes. In a medium bowl, whisk together broth, tomato paste, wine, brandy, and pepper. Pour over duck mixture and stir gently to combine.

6. In a medium bowl, toss bread crumbs, chopped parsley, and melted butter. Sprinkle half of bread crumb mixture evenly over top of casserole.

7. Bake, uncovered, for 45 minutes. Remove from oven and stir top crust into beans. Sprinkle remaining bread crumb mixture over casserole and bake for 45 minutes more, until crust is formed and well browned and beans are tender. Serve right away.

Advance Preparation: Casserole may be made ahead through step 5, covered tightly, and refrigerated overnight or up to 24 hours. Bring to room temperature before baking. Stir in 1 to 2 cups of warm water to moisten.

1 serving: 732 calories, 47 g protein, 37 g total fat (14.4 g saturated), 45 g carbohydrates, 796 mg sodium, 146 mg cholesterol, 14 g dietary fiber

PIZZA POTPIE

MAKES 16 SERVINGS

Anyone who likes pizza will be crazy about this fun casserole—typical pizza ingredients baked under a delicious pizza crust, perfect for a big party.

- 6 cups pizza sauce (recipe follows)
- 2 tablespoons olive oil
- ¼ teaspoon crushed red pepper
- 2 pounds hot Italian sausage, cut into 1-inch pieces
- 2 pounds sweet Italian sausage, cut into 1-inch pieces
- 5 large eggs
- 3 cups part-skim ricotta cheese
- ¾ cup freshly grated Parmesan cheese (3 ounces)
- ⅓ cup chopped fresh basil leaves or 2 tablespoons dried, crumbled
- 3 tablespoons chopped fresh oregano leaves or 1 tablespoon dried, crumbled
- ½ teaspoon freshly ground black pepper
- 6 cups shredded part-skim mozzarella cheese (1 ½ pounds)
- ¾ pound pepperoni, thinly sliced
- 2 pounds refrigerated pizza dough

PREP TIME: 50 MIN + 50 MIN TO MAKE SAUCE
BAKE TIME: 35–45 MIN
STAND TIME: 20 MIN

1. Make one recipe of Pizza Sauce.

2. Meanwhile, in a small bowl, combine oil and red pepper flakes. Set aside.

3. In a large heavy skillet, cook sausages in batches over medium heat, stirring frequently, for 10 minutes, until browned. Using a slotted spoon, transfer to a large bowl. Stir in pizza sauce and set aside.

4. In a large bowl, whisk 4 eggs until frothy. Stir in ricotta, Parmesan cheese, basil, oregano, and pepper.

5. Spoon half of sausage mixture into a shallow 6-quart casserole or roasting pan. Spoon small dollops of ricotta mixture over sauce. Sprinkle with half of mozzarella. Arrange pepperoni over cheese. Repeat with remaining sauce, ricotta mixture, and mozzarella.

6. Preheat oven to 375°F. On a lightly floured surface, roll out three-fourths of dough about ¼ inch thick. Trim to shape of your casserole but 1 inch larger.

7. Place dough over filling, turn edges under, and crimp. Whisk remaining egg with 1 tablespoon water and brush some over dough.

8. Roll out remaining dough and cut out decorative shapes with small cookie cutters. Arrange shapes on top of crust and brush with remaining egg mixture.

9. Brush crust with reserved pepper-olive oil mixture. Bake pie, uncovered, for 35 to 45 minutes, until top is golden brown and filling is heated through. Remove from oven and let cool on a wire rack for 20 minutes before cutting.

Advance Preparation: Casserole may be made ahead through step 8, covered tightly, and refrigerated overnight or up to 24 hours. Bring to room temperature before baking.

1 serving: 746 calories, 44 g protein, 44 g total fat (14.3 g saturated), 44 g carbohydrates, 2,111 mg sodium, 169 mg cholesterol, 4 g dietary fiber

PIZZA SAUCE

MAKES 6 CUPS

PREP TIME: 10 MINUTES · COOK TIME: 40 MINUTES

1 ½ tablespoons olive oil
1 large yellow onion, finely chopped (1 ½ cups)
1 medium red bell pepper, seeded and finely chopped (1 cup)
2 large garlic cloves, minced
2 28-ounce cans Italian-style tomato puree

1 4-ounce can sliced black olives drained
2 tablespoons chopped fresh oregano leaves or 2 teaspoons dried, crumbled
1 tablespoon chopped fresh basil leaves or 1 teaspoon dried, crumbled
1 large bay leaf
Freshly ground black pepper to taste

1. In a large saucepan, heat oil over medium heat. Add onion, bell pepper, and garlic and sauté until onion is soft, about 5 minutes. Stir in tomato puree, olives, oregano, basil, bay leaf, and pepper.
2. Cover and bring to a boil over medium-high heat, stirring frequently. Reduce heat and simmer, partially covered, for 30 minutes, stirring occasionally. Discard bay leaf.

1/2 cup serving: 88 calories, 3 g protein, 3 g total fat (0.4 g saturated), 16 g carbohydrates, 591 mg sodium, 0 cholesterol, 4 g dietary fiber

COUNTRY MACARONI AND CHEESE

MAKES 12 SERVINGS

Macaroni and cheese is only as good as the cheese it's made with. Here I teamed my favorite sharp Cheddar with Colby cheese, a cousin of Cheddar that was first made in the central Wisconsin town of Colby in 1874. It was thirty-three years earlier when European immigrants, homesteading in the Heartland, started Wisconsin's cheese industry. A woman by the name of Anne Pickett is credited with starting the first cottage industry cheese factory in 1841, using milk from neighbors' cows. Today there are more than 160 cheese factories in the state. I prefer to use tubular macaroni such as rigatoni or ziti when I make this casserole, although you can always use the smaller elbow or tiny shells.

2 pounds dried rigatoni or ziti macaroni
¼ cup (½ stick) butter
1 medium yellow onion, finely chopped (1 cup)
1 large garlic clove, minced
¼ cup unbleached all-purpose flour
6 cups whole milk
2 teaspoons Dijon-style mustard
¼ teaspoon cayenne pepper
   Salt, optional, and freshly ground black pepper to taste

3 cups shredded sharp Cheddar cheese (¾ pound)
3 cups shredded Colby cheese (¾ pound)

SPICY TOPPING

3 tablespoons butter
1 small yellow onion, finely chopped (½ cup)
1 large garlic clove, minced
¾ cup dry unseasoned bread crumbs
2 tablespoons minced fresh flat-leaf parsley
½ teaspoon crushed red pepper or to taste

PREP TIME: 40 MIN
BAKE TIME: 25–30 MIN

1. In a large pot, cook macaroni according to package directions. Drain well and return to pot.
2. Meanwhile, preheat oven to 375°F. Butter a deep 5-quart casserole and set aside. In a large deep skillet, melt butter over medium heat. Add onion and garlic and sauté until onion is soft, about 5 minutes. Using a slotted spoon, add onion and garlic to macaroni.
3. Whisk flour into skillet until smooth. Slowly whisk in milk and cook over low heat, whisking constantly, until thickened and smooth, about 5 minutes. Stir in mustard, cayenne, salt, if desired, and pepper. Gradually add cheeses, whisking until melted and mixture is smooth.
4. Pour cheese sauce over macaroni and stir gently to combine. Transfer mixture to prepared casserole.
5. **To make topping:** In a small skillet, melt butter over medium heat. Add onion and garlic and sauté until onion is soft, about 5 minutes. Stir in bread crumbs, parsley, and red pepper flakes. Cook, stirring constantly, until crumbs are lightly coated, about 1 minute. Sprinkle mixture evenly over casserole.
6. Bake casserole, uncovered, for 25 to 30 minutes, until top is golden brown and center of the dish is hot and bubbly. Serve warm.

Advance Preparation: Casserole may be made ahead through step 4, covered tightly, and refrigerated overnight or up to 24 hours. Bring to room temperature before topping and baking.

1 serving: 616 calories, 27 g protein, 30 g total fat (17.4 g saturated), 74 g carbohydrates, 596 mg sodium, 86 mg cholesterol, 3 g dietary fiber

JANSSON'S TEMPTATION

MAKES 12 SERVINGS

This recipe was given to me years ago by a neighbor whose Swedish husband grew up on a Illinois farm, about twenty miles southeast of Bishop Hill, the community where this creamy scalloped potato dish is thought to have originated. Some people claim the dish was named for Erik Jansson, a religious leader who founded an enclave in Bishop Hill in 1846. Legend says that although Jansson preached against giving in to earthly pleasures, this dish was too tempting even for him. My friend served it at the smorgasbord dinner she held every Christmas for neighbors. It makes a wonderful addition to a buffet supper since it's quite good even if it cools to room temperature. Swedish cooks would use marinated sprats in this recipe, a cousin of the herring, but they are difficult to find unless you live near a Swedish-owned market. I've found that anchovies work quite well if they are first soaked in milk to tame their salty flavor.

2 2-ounce cans oil-packed anchovy fillets, drained
½ cup whole milk
6 tablespoons (¾ stick) butter
4 small yellow onions, thinly sliced (2 cups)

8 large russet potatoes (about 4 pounds), peeled
Freshly ground black pepper to taste
2 cups heavy cream
¾ cup dry unseasoned bread crumbs
Chopped fresh parsley for garnish, optional

PREP TIME:
20 MIN + 30 MIN
TO SOAK
ANCHOVIES
BAKE TIME:
1 1/4–1 1/2 HR
STAND TIME:
5 MIN

1. Separate anchovy fillets and place in a shallow nonreactive dish. Pour milk over anchovies, cover, and let stand at room temperature for 30 minutes.

2. Meanwhile, in a large skillet, melt 4 tablespoons butter over medium heat. Add onions and sauté until golden but not browned, about 10 minutes.

3. Preheat oven to 350°F. Lightly butter a shallow 4-quart casserole and set aside. Drain anchovies and discard milk. Finely chop anchovies and set aside.

4. Using a sharp knife or a mandoline slicer, cut potatoes into 2 x ¼-inch sticks (like french fries). Arrange half of potatoes over bottom of prepared casserole. Season with pepper. Top with onions and anchovies, evenly distributing bits of anchovy. Cover with remaining potatoes and season with pepper. Pour in cream and sprinkle with bread crumbs. Dot with remaining 2 tablespoons butter.

5. Place casserole on a large baking sheet. Bake, uncovered, for 1 ¼ to 1 ½ hours, until potatoes are tender and top is golden brown. Let stand for 5 minutes before serving. Sprinkle with chopped parsley, if desired.

1 serving: 337 calories, 6 g protein, 21 g total fat (12.9 g saturated), 32 g carbohydrates, 310 mg sodium, 74 mg cholesterol, 3 g dietary fiber

OZARK PUDDING

MAKES 12 SERVINGS

During the Truman administration, Fulton, Missouri, about ninety miles west of St. Louis, was the site of the summer White House. This dessert is reported to have been a favorite of the late president Harry Truman and the dessert served to Winston Churchill when he came to Fulton to make his famous "Iron Curtain" speech. A delightful ending to any meal, this cakelike pudding makes an excellent portable dessert. The addition of a small amount of unflavored gelatin stabilizes the whipped cream topping so it holds its shape on the dessert table. Since black walnuts are a product of Missouri, I decided to use them in my version of the recipe. Black walnuts are available by mail order (see Sources, page 142), or you can substitute English walnuts or pecans.

1 cup unbleached all-purpose flour
3 ¾ teaspoons baking powder
½ teaspoon salt
3 large eggs
2 ¼ cups granulated sugar
3 large apples such as Jonathan, Rome, or Prairie Spy, peeled, cored, and chopped (3 cups)
1 ½ cups chopped black walnuts
1 tablespoon vanilla extract

WHIPPED CREAM TOPPING

¾ teaspoon unflavored gelatin
1 ½ tablespoons cold water
1 ½ cups heavy cream
3 tablespoons confectioners' sugar
1 ½ teaspoons vanilla extract
2 tablespoons dark rum, Grand Marnier, or Cointreau, optional

PREP TIME: 30 MIN

BAKE TIME: 30 MIN

1. Preheat oven to 325°F. Lightly butter a shallow 3-quart casserole and set aside. Chill medium bowl for topping in step 5.

2. On a sheet of waxed paper, sift together flour, baking powder, and salt. In a medium bowl, whisk together eggs and granulated sugar until pale and fluffy. Stir in flour mixture until blended. Stir in apples, walnuts, and 1 tablespoon vanilla. Spoon mixture into prepared casserole.

3. Bake, uncovered, for 30 minutes, until top is nicely browned and a tester inserted into center comes out clean. Remove from oven and cool on a wire rack.

4. **Meanwhile, make topping:** In a small custard dish, sprinkle gelatin over water and let stand for 5 minutes to soften. Place dish in a small skillet filled with hot water and heat over medium heat, stirring constantly, until gelatin is clear and completely dissolved, about 3 minutes. Remove dish from water and set aside to cool to room temperature (do not allow to cool too much, or gelatin will begin to set).

5. Pour cream into the chilled bowl. Using an electric mixer, beat on medium speed until cream begins to thicken. While beating, slowly pour in dissolved gelatin. Then beat in confectioners' sugar, vanilla, and rum, if using. Beat until well blended and cream falls into soft mounds when beaters are lifted. With a hand-held whisk, whisk until cream thickens and holds its shape when beater is lifted. Transfer whipped cream to a serving bowl and chill until ready to serve.

6. To serve, spoon pudding into dessert bowls. Spoon whipped cream over each serving.

1 serving: 436 calories, 7 g protein, 21 g total fat (7.8 g saturated), 56 g carbohydrates, 269 mg sodium, 94 mg cholesterol, 2 g dietary fiber

CHOCOLATE BREAD PUDDING

MAKES 16 SERVINGS

This recipe comes from a church cookbook published by my mother's "Stitch and Chat" group in 1958. The recipe is so worn with use that the name of the provider is no longer legible, but I've been grateful over the years to the unknown woman who submitted it. It's delicious. The pudding should seem underbaked. Serve this delectable treat as the grand finale to any festive buffet, year-round. Offer the confectioners' sugar in an antique shaker to sprinkle over each serving.

1 unsliced loaf (1 pound) home-style white bread, cut into 1-inch cubes (12 cups)
3 cups heavy cream
2 cups whole milk
½ pound bittersweet chocolate, finely chopped
½ pound semisweet chocolate, finely chopped

6 large eggs
1 ¼ cups sugar
1 tablespoon vanilla extract
⅔ cup chopped walnuts
Pinch of salt
Confectioners' sugar for garnish, optional

PREP TIME: 35 MIN

BAKE TIME: 40–50 MIN

1. Preheat oven to 325°F. Lightly butter a shallow 4-quart casserole and set aside. Put the bread cubes in a large bowl.

2. In a large saucepan, bring cream and milk just to a boil over medium heat. Reduce heat and gradually add chocolates, stirring until melted and mixture is smooth. Pour mixture over bread and stir gently to combine. Set aside.

3. In a large bowl, whisk eggs until frothy. Whisk in sugar and vanilla. Stir in walnuts and salt. Pour over bread and stir gently to combine.

4. Transfer bread mixture to prepared casserole. Smooth evenly with back of a spoon. Cover with aluminum foil and bake for 40 to 50 minutes, until edges are firm but center is still moist. Serve warm with a sprinkling of confectioners' sugar, if desired.

1 serving: 519 calories, 10 g protein, 34 g total fat (17.6 g saturated), 49 g carbohydrates, 197 mg sodium, 146 mg cholesterol, 2 g dietary fiber

SOURCES

AMERICAN SPOON FOODS
(dried cherries, dried cranberries, and morels)
P.O. Box 566
Petoskey, MI 49770–0556
(800) 222–5886

FOREST RESOURCE CENTER
(shiitake mushrooms)
Route 2, Box 156A
Lanesboro, MN 55949
(507) 467–2437

MAYTAG DAIRY FARMS
(Maytag blue cheese)
P.O. Box 806
Newton, IA 50208
(800) 247–2458

MISSOURI DANDY PANTRY
(black walnuts)
P.O. Box A
414 North Street
Stockton, MO 65785
(800) 872–6879

MOZE'S GOURMET SPECIALTIES
(wild rice)
2701 Monroe St.
Madison, WI 53711
(800) 369–7423

SEED SAVER'S EXCHANGE
(information on obtaining seeds for heirloom vegetables)
3076 North Winn Road
Decorah, IA 52101
(319) 382–5990

WILD GAME AND THE HERB PURVEYOR INC.
(pheasant and duck breasts)
2315 West Huron St.
Chicago, IL 60612
(312) 278–1661

INDEX